Real Men Wear Beige

Real Men Wear Beige

ONE MAN'S JAILHOUSE JOURNEY THROUGH THE
CHAOTIC REALM OF CONCRETE AND STEEL

Donato Alfredano

www.rmwbeige.com

© 2015 Donato Alfredano. All rights reserved.

ISBN: 1516920880
ISBN 13: 9781516920884
Library of Congress Control Number: 2015913444
CreateSpace Independent Publishing Platform
North Charleston, South Carolina

Disclaimer
This book is based on a true story. While all the events and depictions in this book are true, names, locations, dates, and other identifying details have been changed to protect the privacy of the people involved. The events are portrayed to the best of the author's memory. In some cases, the author has compressed events; in others, he has expanded on them. The events in this book are based on firsthand knowledge and experience with some exceptions, where the author has interjected secondhand information to form a cohesive portrayal of events.

The extrapolations and opinions shared in this book are solely those of the author. They are not meant to imply or represent factual conclusions, nor are they predicated on any official determinations, documents, or declarations.

The information provided in this book is for explanatory purposes only and is not intended as legal guidance.

Dedication

This book is dedicated to the loving memory of my sister, C. G. Throughout my life, she was my rock in times of need and my inspiration in times of heartache. Her face and her voice will forever be ingrained in my soul.

Table of Contents

Acknowledgments · ix

Introduction· xi

Chapter 1 Solitude Is Bliss ·1

Chapter 2 "Who Done It" ·15

Chapter 3 The Grand Entrance ·49

Chapter 4 Real Men Wear Beige ·97

About the Author ·129

Acknowledgments

I wish to acknowledge my very best friend and the sweetest, most loving and generous person I have ever known. "Ti amo Matilde."
I wish to acknowledge my dear wife and family for their unwavering love and support throughout those dark days before, during, and after my prison journey.

Real Men Wear Beige has corresponding Soundtrack, excerpts of which can be heard on the Audible version of the book. The full Soundtrack is available at www.rmwbeige.com. The project was recorded by Paul Orofino at Millbrook Sound Studio, NY, and mixed by Michael James and Roey Shamir. It includes performances by the following guest artists:

Corey Glover (of Living Colour), Paul Pesco (of Hall & Oates, Madonna, & Britney Spears), Andy Snitzer, Kent Smith and Michael Davis (the horn section for The Rolling Stones, 1994 to 1997), Jay Dittamo (of the Band from Utopia), Ron Bienstock, Esq (of Blue East & JT Jazz Collective), Karl Alweir, and our author and songwriter, Don Alfredano.

Introduction

"Prison." "Jail." "Incarceration." What comes to mind when people think of these words? What comes to mind when they think of our criminal justice system? There is a dictionary's worth of words that flash through the average person's mind—words and terms like "penitentiary," "the slammer," "big house," or "the pokey."

How about prison inmates? In all probability, the words that come to mind include "delinquents," "criminals," "felons," or "gangsters." Or maybe you're one of those who prefers "dirt bags," "scum of the earth," or some other choice derogatory term for those supposedly disgusting outcasts of society. Is there even one positive thing that comes to mind when people think of prison? I'll bet I'm 99 percent accurate in saying the answer is no. Yet what do people really *know* about prison and the criminal justice system?

Unlike most other things in life, for which people can formulate opinions and pass judgment based on experience and familiarization, prison is essentially an enigma to the "average Joe." Other than what they see in movies and on television, they have no realistic idea of how the criminal justice system truly functions, what daily life in prison is actually like, and, most importantly, just *who* criminals are.

My point is this: it's natural that we all think about prison and jail in the negative sense because, arguably, it is a place for people who have either wronged society or broken some rules. Yes, naturally, the punitive nature of prison fosters thoughts of retribution and revulsion in all of us to some degree or another. However, what we so easily forget to consider is, in actuality, the core of the matter—and that is *humanity*. Damned right. It's all about people. Not just *other* people, but people like your son or daughter, mother or father, sister, brother, or friend.

We deal with the idea of prison the same way we deal with cancer. We merely latch on to complacency and focus on the reassuring notion that "it could never happen to me." This natural defense mechanism is simply our way of shielding ourselves from life's harsh realities. That, in and of itself, is not necessarily a bad thing. However, if we stop there, enlightenment and empathy are absent, and we stand to learn nothing. From the perspective of someone who has spent a little bit of time behind those concrete walls and steel bars, I'm going to reveal some hard, cold facts about prison life through my expressive and provocative story. That's right—"Been there, done that, and got the T-shirt." Of course, I'm talking about the orange DOC (Department of Corrections) T-shirt.

My hope is that my story will help you to acquire a more accurate and realistic perspective of what incarceration is all about. I want to reveal how people in any setting, whether free or restrained or cast into the most abrasive of circumstances, are incredibly consistent. In terms of the illustrations and opinions of our criminal justice system and our sentencing process, just apply your common sense and consider the facts, not only as they are conveyed in this book, but in general. Then, and only then, will you be able to draw reasonable and accurate conclusions.

Let's break the world of incarceration down a bit further. On one side, there are the hard, cold realities of the chaotic world of being convicted and incarcerated that we so strongly despise. On the other side, there are the understated, virtuous moralities that we all embrace so strongly. Well, in prison, when both sides come together, they form the most bizarre, sometimes amusing, and sometimes ironic examples of plain, old, unadulterated humanity.

Some of what you read in this book will support your preconceived notions of prison and our criminal justice system, and it'll be just like what you've read in the newspaper or seen on TV. But I'll bet that most of what I tell you will surprise or even shock you—and maybe make you start thinking about prison and justice a little differently. I hope it does just that.

CHAPTER 1
Solitude Is Bliss

The Zach Attack

It was a cold winter, circa 2004. It was about 7:00 p.m. on the tier at Rikers Island, New York City's main jail complex. It sits on a four-hundred-acre island in the East River, between Queens and the Bronx.

We'd just finished dinner. Normally, everyone would be settling into their favorite spot and doing their thing, whatever that happened to be. But this night was different.

There was tension in the air as guys were trying to hide what they knew was about to happen. For days, plans were being made by a group of guys to mount a 7:30 p.m. surprise attack on Zach and his buddies—about eight of them. It was covertly being called "the Zach Attack." Just about everyone knew about the planned offensive, and most had either picked sides or placed bets or both.

Zach was a smart-assed little prick—you know, one of those punks who pranced around lapping it up as if they were at summer camp or in high-school gym class. He was constantly pushing everyone's buttons and often ended up getting his ass kicked for it. But he wouldn't quit. No matter how many times he got smacked around, he'd go back and start the same shit all over again. He eventually managed to put together a gang of heavy hitters who hung out with him and helped protect him: a combo of black, white, and Latino outcasts desperate enough to pair up with him. Zach reminded me of a ten-year-old who keeps asking questions, and even after you answer him, he continues to ask, "Why, what for, and how come?" just to bug you. To me he was simply annoying, but there were others who absolutely hated him and wanted to do him some serious harm.

The "big hand" inched down toward seven-thirty on the caged, gymnasium-style clock on the back wall of the tier as everyone hung around trying to act as inconspicuously as possible—a little too hard, I think. The air was so thick that one of the correction officers (COs) asked me and my buddies what the hell was going on. In fact, at 7:29 p.m., it got crazy quiet—so quiet that the same CO was beginning to stammer into his radio, "I got a code five, blah, blah…. Things don't feel right in here. I'm gonna need—" And before he even finished his sentence, the rampage began.

The first blow was a kick to Zach's head as he and his buddies were sitting on the floor against the wall playing cards. He didn't see it coming. It was solid, and it was brutal. Zach's gang was at a great disadvantage because they were all on the floor, giving their assailants (about ten of them all together) the ability to kick and beat them as they struggled to stand up. None of them even had much of a chance to fight back. More guys jumped in on both sides, but it was an easy two-to-one ratio against Zach's gang. Yes, it was a slaughter-fest that felt as if it lasted forever, but in reality lasted only about two minutes from start to finish.

A steady flow of COs began rushing into the tier, but the onslaught was practically over before they were able to do much about it. Toward the end of this mini-massacre, Zach made his way up off the floor with his face full of cuts and blood and attempted to get away from the beating. Have you ever seen someone who was knocked so senseless that he couldn't walk a straight line? I'll never forget it. He was actually walking sideways, one foot over the other, with his arms out to keep his balance. Then, to top it all off, Zach made it only about ten feet before someone came up from behind him and hit him with one last blow to the head, which knocked him unconscious, and he collapsed over a lunch table. The whole thing was gruesome and sad.

Sure, everyone knows incarceration has its horrifying moments and shocking events, but times like these always made me sick…and I mean literally. I'm not just talking about witnessing someone getting brutally beaten; I'm talking about the guys who got off on watching it happen. Jumping around, cheering, and howling like a pack of wolves over their wounded prey. Being in prison made me realize for the first time in my life how little difference there can be between man and beast. At the core of our existence, we share that "pack of wolves," gang-style mentality. There are those who prey upon and devour the weak, the disadvantaged, and as in Zack's case, those whom they just don't like. I just wasn't cut out for this kind of crap. In time, it would become clear to me that I was in the prison minority on the issue.

We were locked down for twenty-four hours and then twenty-four more as the authorities tried to run through the videotapes and figure out who to throw in the hole and who to sack with criminal charges. Lockdown meant that once a day, two of us at a time could leave our eight-by-ten cells for long enough to walk to the bathroom, stand around for twenty minutes, and go back to our cell again. There seemed to be no such thing as a thermostat at Rikers. Twenty four-seven, you felt like a piece of slimy fried chicken being dipped in a deep fryer. That meant forty-eight long hours of sweat, stink, and a whole lot of silence. Yeah, you run out of things to talk about after the first twelve hours, and after the second twelve, you don't even care.

It may be a cliché to say, but during times like these, I tried hard to think positive and focus on inspirational thoughts. I thought about things like this quote I once heard by Laurence Sterne: "In solitude, the mind gains strength and learns to lean upon itself." Prison made me believe this was absolutely true. Yes, the mind's amazing ability to endure and overcome relentless emotional pain and suffering is nothing short of a miracle. And I haven't stopped searching for miracles. So, just like a child, I guess I still believe in them.

It's been years since those dark and dirty days in lockdown. Life has been good to me, and I've moved on. However, it was behind prison walls that I learned some of the most extraordinary lessons about life and humanity. These life lessons are now ingrained in my heart and soul. And yes, when the lights go down, I still support the notion that "solitude is bliss."

The Perfect Storm

Most people don't really put together that there is a nexus among large groups of people, regardless of the institution. Prison is no different. I once heard someone say that chaos is order yet undeciphered. How true it is. You put any large group of individuals under the same roof, or on the same campus or base of operation, and there will most certainly be some level of chaos. Whether it's a prison, college, or the military, for that matter, the same equation applies. Just for fun, let's see what the equation might look like.

Here are the variables: Personalities (*P*), Rules (*R*), Responsibilities (*Re*), Oppression (*O*), and Desperation (*D*), with the common denominator being Humanity (*H*). So:

$$(H / P) \times (R + Re) = (C) \text{ and } C = \text{chaos}$$

Now, when chaos is multiplied by oppression and desperation (*O* ± *D*), two more elements that permeate throughout the prison system, the equation might look something like this:

$$(H / P) \times (R + Re) = (C) (O \pm D) = \text{The perfect storm}$$

Yes, now we've created what I'm calling "the perfect storm." That's prison.

For all intents and purposes, our little equation is just a fun way of illustrating how prison, jail, incarceration, or whatever you want to call it—is synonymous with chaos. A microcosm of the best and the worst of society live and breathe behind the walls of prison, from the dregs to the divine. You know, I met some of the worst and best people I had ever known while I was incarcerated. I met some of the dumbest and smartest ones, too. After I was released and I'd say that to people, they would look at me as if I were completely crazy. It never really occurred to them that you could meet the "best" or "smartest" people you had ever known *in a prison*, but it's true. For every screwed-up, slimy piece of shit I encountered, there was a surprising number of decent, generous, normal guys just trying to survive the hellhole they'd been thrown into. In the coming pages, you'll get a good sense of these diversities in terms of personalities, attitudes, humanities, and daily life.

What's It All About?

I was no "spring chicken" when I was ensnared by the long arms of the law. I was about fifty years old, with absolutely no criminal record. Except for a few hours in a holding cell in California when I was twenty-one on a warrant for unpaid speeding tickets, I had never seen the inside of a jail cell. I was a "first offender." I'm sure you've heard the term.

Not counting my initial adventure through the New York criminal justice system and a brief stint on the world-famous Rikers Island, which I'll talk about later, I spent about six months in county jail before I was sentenced and shipped off to state prison. I was accused of a white-collar crime, which in my home state and in my particular case was classified as a second-degree felony by statute. When you've been arrested for a crime, sometimes by way of a grand jury decision, you are placed in jail until you are sentenced. After you are sentenced, you go to state or federal prison, dependent on whether you broke a state or federal law. Here's a simple, but important, distinction between jail and prison: "The most notable difference is that prison inmates have been tried and convicted of crimes, while those in jail may be awaiting trial. A prison is under the jurisdiction of either federal or state, while the jail holds people accused under federal, state, county, and/or city laws. A jail holds detainees from two days up to one year."[1]

For clarity, here's an important distinction to remember: If you are in jail awaiting trial, you are called a "detainee," not an "inmate." Inmates are those who have already been tried, sentenced, and sent to prison.

In jail, you're just another "small cog in a very large wheel." While I was incarcerated, I used to think of it as a cattle call because that's what it feels like when you're living it. Everyone is rounded up like a big herd of cattle and placed in their pen, all the while being prodded, kicked in the ass, and put into place—sometimes figuratively and sometimes actually. Some remain for a few days and some for up to a year, but they're all waiting to be put out to pasture and given the freedom to roam, or be handed over to the meat factory, better known as the DOC (department of corrections). Yep, they're the ones who run our prison system.

Then there are the courts. The misguided notion many people have is that the courtroom is the altar of righteousness. It's not only where you are tried, but judgment is cast upon you, and you receive your sentence and find out where justice is to be served. Well, here's a revelation for you: maybe it is, and maybe it isn't. To say the least, justice is a highly subjective matter. If you don't believe this, then I'm glad you're reading this book because it might be time for a little reality check.

---

1 Diffen, "Jail vs. Prison, Difference," http://www.diffen.com/difference/Jail_vs_Prison.

DONATO ALFREDANO

Did Someone Say "Reality Check"?

Let's get right to the point. Is justice alive and well in the United States? Comparatively speaking, of course it is. After all, we are not a Third-World country. However, nothing is perfect, and judging from my personal experience, there is a gaping hole that permeates our justice system, which is, for the most part, ignored. It lives and breathes in our often inequitable sentencing process. For every asshole behind bars who deserves to be there, there are just as many who don't. And for every asshole who has been sentenced in accordance with the law to a reasonable number of years in prison, there are just as many who have been slammed by the system and become victims of bad circumstances and internal politics.

A spider web comes to mind—some get away, and some get caught in the fray. The outcome is relatively indiscriminate. Like most everyone else, I never really gave a damn about this issue until I had the misfortune of becoming personally entangled in my own spider web. My incarceration afforded me a bird's-eye view of detainees coming and going like an orange-jumpsuit merry-go-round. I watched the bartering, the "who you know" bullshit, and the glaring inconsistencies in our sentencing process as they unfolded. My experience and analysis, both inside *and* outside of the prison walls, have confirmed to me the glaring contrast of principles often demonstrated by those who administer our sentencing laws.

To validate the argument, let's look at two straightforward examples right out of my handy-dandy prison logbook.

Once upon a time, there were two Italian guys named Ike. The first inmate was named Ike Gotoffizzi. He was a white male, thirty-five years old, accused of molesting a ten-year-old girl. It was his fourth offense, and there was an eyewitness account. His sentence: three years.

Wait a minute. What? That bastard could be out on parole in about eleven months in most states! You don't how many times I watched these freaking child predators walk out of county jail, never seeing the likes of state prison, after being accused of molesting some poor kid or doing some other heinous thing to them. That's not justice. That's just plain old immoral.

Now, the second inmate was named Ike Gotscrootti. He was a white male, forty-six years old, accused of theft by deception of $20,000. It was his first offense. He was sentenced to six years.

Wait a minute. What? This poor bastard is going to prison longer than the asshole who just molested a little girl? That's right. I sat in prison with guys who were there for drug possession, minor assault, embezzlement charges, and lesser crimes, who received sentences of five to ten years, while a ton of other sick bastards like Mr. Ike Gotoffizzi walked.

Granted, those are two stark examples of flawed sentencing, but they are nonetheless quite real, especially to the guy sitting behind those bars. You know, after having witnessed this kind of lopsided justice day in and day out, I don't know if I could do a prosecutor's job—or a public defender's (PD's) job, for that matter. For every scumbag you put away for good reason, you end up sending some other poor bastard to prison who really didn't deserve the sentence he got.

I'm not trying to bash prosecutors and PDs. I know they're just doing a job. But having experienced incarceration firsthand, I just don't know if I could sleep at night knowing the kind of hellhole I was about to send some not-so-guilty individual to for five times longer than he actually deserves, while at the same time, I'm unable to procure any more than a disgustingly short sentence for some scumbag child molester.

Now, "prosecutorial discretion" is a term worthy of mention. "Prosecutorial discretion" refers to the fact that under American law, prosecuting attorneys have nearly absolute power to decide whether or not to bring criminal charges and what those charges will be, as long as there is evidence to support them. Yes, the expectation is that a prosecutor will handle every case in a fair and objective manner. However, for a number of reasons that are beyond the scope of this chapter, instead of "objectivity," subjectivity rears its ugly head, and "fair and objective" become vindictive and skewed in our criminal justice system. And the prosecutor is not always the one who is directly at fault. Politics, principles, allies, enemies, and money are all at play.

Do you know what really pisses me off? People throw numbers of years around like fucking marbles. They'll say, "Give him ten years!" as if they're talking about bananas or something. Believe me, one year of prison is like five in the free world. Now, here's a fun idea: I've often thought that as a prerequisite to becoming a judge or prosecutor, you should be required to actually spend a few fucking months in prison. Then you would have some realistic gauge of what you're doing when you dole out a sentence and what one year behind bars really means. Of course, I'm not being serious, but I'm sure you get my point.

As I said earlier, to me it is troubling how human nature compels us to think very little about prison and our system of justice. We just block it out of our minds. I guess some people think our criminal justice and prison systems are infallible simply because it's what they want to believe. Still others acknowledge its flaws but impulsively chalk it up to being a necessary evil. Really? I'm OK with the evil part, but not the necessary part. If it's a system that can be changed for the better, then it should be changed for the better. Just like any other regulatory agency, or judicial body, or law of the land, when the system is broken, we attempt to fix it. We do our best to modify and amend our laws to make them better. A "necessary" evil would be one that truly cannot or should not be changed. Our criminal justice system is not one of them.

Until it actually hits home, and until it actually involves our sister, brother, boyfriend, husband, or ourselves, we take on a "Who gives a shit? They got what they deserved" attitude toward the issue. I get that, but it is undoubtedly worth some small effort to improve the quality of justice. It certainly would be if *you* were the one on trial. I can tell you that being sentenced to prison is the last thing in the world I ever thought could happen to me—but it did. Let's be clear—I'm not talking about a bunch of "prison reform" or "prison overcrowding" crap here. I'm simply talking about reconciling the subjectivity and imbalance in our sentencing process. Come on, people! The punishment should fit the crime—plain and simple. It's not rocket science.

Oh, by the way, in our example, who should be released first? Who do you want sitting in the same room with your ten-year-old daughter: Mr. Ike Gotoffizzi or Mr. Ike Gotscrootti?

Kool-Aid Wars

I was fairly new to incarceration when I learned that there seemed to be no limit to the things people were willing to fight about. In addition, as you might imagine in jail, sometimes having way too much time on your hands makes little problems seem like huge ones.

At county jail, we ate our meals in a large, open recreation area that housed dozens of metal, picnic-style tables. At each table sat an established group of guys, usually about eight. After getting in line to pick up your food tray, you sat down at your table, and one person was allowed to go back and get the allotted one pitcher of Kool-Aid to bring back for your table. But one or two extra pitchers were always left, which fueled the constant drama over the elusive extra Kool-Aid pitcher and which table was going to end up getting it. Personally, I didn't give a damn about the Kool-Aid dilemma because I hated the stuff and never drank it anyway. But I was getting aggravated with all the drama and constant bullshit floating around about freaking Kool-Aid.

There were a few tables where the black contingent sat. They always seemed to find a way of finagling a second pitcher of Kool-Aid for their group. This pissed all the other groups off to no end. As the days passed, the pressure was building and approaching a boiling point. One of the guys at my table started hyperventilating and chanting under his breath, "I'm gonna kill 'em, I'm gonna kill them black SOBs," over and over again.

Soon, everyone at the table was chiming in with a variety of choice words and phrases about ass kicking and Kool-Aid. *Oh geez, here we fucking go. The shit is about to hit the fan*, I thought as the tension built to a crescendo. Then I did something totally out of character. I was fairly new to the tier, but I was about to make my first bold move. Some kind of warped paternal instinct kicked in, and I took a very big risk.

I stood up, walked over to one of the tables of black dudes, who, by the way, were getting off on the hostility coming from our table and smirking back at our enraged group of guys. I forced a smile on my face and said, "What's up, guys? Yesterday, and the day before, and the day before that, you guys got the extra Kool-Aid. Now it's our turn. That's why I'm going to pick up that pitcher of Kool-Aid and walk back to my table with it, and you guys aren't going to stop me. Right?"

A few of them jumped up from their table, getting ready to grab me as I stood there for a few seconds with the pitcher of Kool-Aid in my hand. But to my absolute surprise, so did my table and about five other tables on the tier, making the point that everyone had had enough of the Kool-Aid-mongering routine, and they were ready to fight about it. Being massively outnumbered, the black contingent sat down and began eating their dinner as if nothing happened.

As I slowly walked back to my table, I looked back and noticed one of the black dudes watching me and nodding his head in what appeared to be approval of what I'd done. I wasn't sure what this was all about and just let it go. My heart was beating out of my chest, and I could hardly swallow my food as I sat there pretending that what I had done was "no big deal." But it was. My actions that day were a "spur of the moment" reaction to the annoying ignorance and pettiness I felt swirling around me, but they could have gotten me slaughtered. It was definitely not a wise decision.

However, two positive things did come from my unwise decision. One, I had earned a good amount of respect from the tier for stepping up to the plate, and two, I inadvertently made friends with one of the guys from the black contingent—the guy whom I saw nodding at me. In the coming months, he would become one of my best friends.

Yep, shortly after the Kool-Aid fiasco, he approached me to say, "Hey brother, that was a brave thing you did, and you did it with respect and self-control. It's great to meet you." Yes, Lonnie would turn out to be a good friend and a ray of light in an otherwise dark and dismal place.

To Bail or Not to Bail

I feel inclined to mention that there is an exception to the rule that everyone automatically stays in a county jail, goes to court for their hearing and sentencing, and gets whisked away to prison if and when they're found guilty. This exception is called "bail." It's like a get-out-of-jail-free card, only it's not quite free. I'm not going to get into the inner workings of bail itself, but the word actually means security, or payment, so if you can afford it, our system allows you to buy some temporary freedom. After you are arrested, taken to jail, and booked, here's a simplified explanation of what's supposed to happen next:

Typically, a first appearance includes these three hearings:

1. **Arraignment:** The prosecutor charges you or provides a complaint. You may enter a plea (guilty or not guilty) at this time, or you may wait until the initial trial appearance. Keep in mind that if you plead guilty, it is impossible to take it back. You may wish to challenge whether there is probable cause. You may demand a

written complaint. (Note: The prosecutor can drop the charges at any time, or the judge can dismiss for lack of probable cause. If the charges are dropped, new charges can be brought later.)
2. **Bail hearing:** Your bail is set or you are released on personal recognizance (meaning you don't pay bail; you just promise to make your court appearances). You or your attorney may present reasons why you can be released safely (such as that you won't flee or be a danger to society). This evidence includes how long you've lived in your community, where you work or go to school, and so on. (Note: If you are from out of state or have outstanding warrants, the judge may set a higher bail.)
3. **Appointment of counsel:** If you can show on paper that you have a low income, you may get a public defender or other free legal representation. You may also hire an attorney or represent yourself (known as *pro se*).

Bail options? If a bail amount is set, you have a few options:

1. You can put up the full bail amount if you have it, which would then be returned to you when your case is over, less any fines or restitution if you plead guilty or are convicted at trial; or
2. If you don't have the full bail amount, you can make an arrangement with a bail bonds agent, which typically involves paying them 10 percent of the total bail amount, plus fees, and putting down collateral for the remaining amount of the bail (for example, the deed to a house). The bail bonds agent then agrees to cover your bail amount for your release, but you do not ever get the money you paid them returned to you.
3. You can have your lawyer fight to get your bail reduced at a future hearing.
4. You can choose not to bail out. This avoids putting up large amounts of money for your bail or losing money to a bail bonds agent.[2]

---

[2] Support Cece McDonald, "Arrest, Jail, and the Court Process," http://supportcece.wordpress.com/legal-info/arrest-jail-court-process/.

In an upcoming chapter, you'll see how I missed an opportunity to use the bail option advantageously. Without a doubt, there are times when bailing out and pulling yourself out of the system, even for a short period of time, might allow you to "get your house in order," talk to your lawyer, prepare for a trial, or do whatever your particular case might require. Statistics show that those who are able to bail out before going to trial and sentencing fare better than those who don't. However, bailing out is not always the smartest choice.

Let's use another one of my examples. After I was arraigned, my bail was set at $220,000, cash only. That meant that I would have to come up with $220,000 cash to get me out on bail—no 10 percent, no real estate, nothing. That's mainly because my lawyer couldn't convince the judge that I wouldn't flee the state. Our counterargument was that I had just returned to the United States for the specific purpose of turning myself in. So does it make sense that I was now going to flee? No, it doesn't, but the judge wouldn't budge. It went in one end of the gavel and out the other. So putting the obvious question aside, which is whether I had $220,000 in cash lying around somewhere or not, there is another thing to consider if you're faced with a conviction.

In other words, if you are guilty and sure you'll be doing some time behind bars, you may want to consider whether you can handle staying in county jail, as opposed to going home on bail. You're probably thinking, *Is this guy nuts? Of course I'd choose bail.* I understand, but hear me out. The time you spend in county jail waiting to be sentenced and eventually sent to prison is counted as part of your upcoming sentence in 99 percent of cases. It's called "time served." Laws differ from state to state regarding how time served is calculated, however, consider the following example: Say you receive a five-year sentence and you've just spent 122 days, or four months, in a county jail. In most states, with a five-year sentence, you can be released on parole after approximately fifteen months. Therefore, fifteen months minus four months equals eleven months. So you'll serve a total of eleven months in prison, not fifteen.

Again, if you're guilty and fairly sure you're going to be sentenced and serve some time, then why not start doing your time and get it over with as soon as possible? That's what I did. It was a tough freaking decision, but it's one that I've never regretted. Sure, you don't want to spend more time in prison than you absolutely have to—ain't that the truth—but, on the other hand, prolonging the inevitable is just plain stupid.

The Yard

It was the day of my jaunt from county jail to state prison, and the intake center was our first stop. This is where you remain until they figure out where they're going to place you after you've been sentenced. I was there for only about a week.

After being schlepped from one disgusting cell to another, I eventually ended up in a cell with a white drug dealer nicknamed Choobie. He was a first-timer like me. We got along well, and I got to like him for his sense of humor and good-natured attitude toward things. He received a seven-year sentence after being implicated and set up, allegedly by his partner in crime. They nabbed him on his way to delivering a large quantity of cocaine to a college sorority house. Must have been some education those ladies were getting.

On this day, we were let outside onto the prison yard for an hour of so-called recreation. Man, this was the stuff that all the prison movies are made of. There had to be four hundred guys out there in the "yard." Some were playing basketball or soccer or lifting weights, and some were just sitting around in small pockets of five and ten, watching the chaotic bunch of activity swirling around them. Choobie and I just walked the perimeter, along with a number of other lost souls who didn't have a group or gang to hang around with. Unlike most of the younger guys, for me this was a choice, not a predicament.

All of a sudden, the shit hit the fan. Two guys ran up to us and started screaming at Choobie and shoving him around. It quickly became clear that they knew him from the streets. He knew he was outnumbered and tried to back away, but they started pounding him before he could even take a few steps. I got the hell out of the way as fast as I could. There was no way I was going to be able to stop these guys who were obviously enraged with enough hatred for Choobie to tear him to shreds, and that's putting it mildly.

As the whole yard descended toward the beating, I could only stand there and watch as these guys beat the holy hell out of Choobie. Like some mindless, faceless creature in a crowd of many, sucked up into the movie screen of some ultraviolent Hollywood production, I stood there with my heart pounding out of my chest. I questioned how I could ever have allowed myself to be cast into this paralyzing world of chaos and violence. It was a repulsively surreal feeling.

About twenty COs swarmed in and eventually calmed things down. They hauled Choobie's bruised and beaten body away, and I never heard from him again. It turned out that he was involved on the outside with his attackers in some kind of drug deal gone bad just months before this sickening day of reckoning. I guess you never know who you're going to meet in prison, and Choobie seemed like a good soul. The world is full of surprises and disappointments, and this was a big one for Choobie…and me.

CHAPTER 2
"Who Done It"

Life's a bitch. For me, maybe more like a roller coaster, and my tempestuous ride landed me behind bars. Without getting into a lot of detail, I was working for the government and was accused of taking money I was not entitled to. Sorry to sound so unglamorous, but what it really boiled down to was that I had been cheating on my expenses.

Based on the details of this particular incident, this is a charge that would probably have been called "theft by deception" in the private sector, but in the public sector, it fell under the purview of official misconduct, a second-degree crime in most states. The dollar amount was relatively low in comparison to most cases you're likely to hear about; let's just say it added up to under $20,000, accumulated over a period of four years. Again, not too glamorous, but it serves to exemplify the irony of my unusual jailhouse journey.

When it finally became clear that a full-blown investigation was underway and there was little doubt that I would be facing charges, my life began to spiral out of control. To say the least, it was the worst phase of my life, both spiritually and emotionally. Alcohol, an affair, domestic issues, and erratic behavior—yes, I was having the classic, textbook meltdown coupled with a severe case of unmanageable midlife crisis. I knew it was inevitable that the shit would eventually hit the fan, and the apprehension was making me completely insane.

To make a bad situation worse, shortly after I was essentially forced to leave my employment, I was informed by an "insider" friend that a scandal was beginning to brew that involved government contracts and $1.5

million. Rumor had it that I was suspected of either stealing or deriving some benefit from these government contracts. This was just a plain old misguided and unsubstantiated case of guilt by association. The screwball thought process was that "if he took that twenty thousand, then that sneaky bastard *must* have finagled the one-point-five mill, too! Yeah, let's get him. Let's give him fifty years. Yeah, yeah!" cried the lynch mob. Man, for a short while, I was being blamed for so many things that I began to wonder if I might actually be responsible for the invasion of Iraq.

Anyway, anyone with half a brain would come to recognize the whole $1.5 million as total bullshit. There was absolutely nothing factual to substantiate the allegation. That being said, I wasn't going to take this rumor too lightly. Who knew what kind of firestorm the authorities might create over this? A million dollars is serious cash, and it implied serious trouble and serious time behind bars. To make things even worse, as you might imagine, I had made a few enemies with some top-level officials during my employment. It was time to go into "defense mode" and decide how best to protect myself.

Fight or Flight

After all, we do live in a culture of accountability, and I was about to swallow a big, fat slice of *mea culpa*. Where I come from, when the going gets tough, the tough get going. I had already taken a job out of state because, for obvious reasons, I could no longer get one in my home state. Then, after receiving an offer to teach in Europe, I left the United States on a little hiatus where I would sit tight and watch long distance as this ridiculous but potentially dangerous escapade played itself out.

I was relieved when, a few months later, my friend back home informed me that the authorities had essentially resolved the $1.5 million mystery, which was eventually determined to be a procedural matter involving the contract bidding law. Of course that, too, was made out to be entirely my fault, but it did not warrant criminal action against me. However, as anticipated, I eventually did get the call from my family saying that I was in the newspaper, front page, being officially charged for "official misconduct."

After a week or so of discussing matters long distance with my lawyer in New York, I decided to just return to the United States and face the charges, now that I knew they didn't include a million-dollar bonus prize. As the story goes, my lawyer had spoken to the prosecutor to inform him that I would be returning to the States to turn myself in. And I did. I purchased my airline ticket, and twelve days after the front-page headline, I was on my way back to the good ole USA. To this day, I do not believe a time span of twelve days was an unreasonable amount of time to wait to turn myself in, and I will always question the expectations of the authorities who, as we will discuss later, seemed to think it was.

As a side note, let's look at the legal implications with regard to logistics. Although they never did come right out and say it, the authorities had no clue where I was. They may have assumed I was somewhere in Europe, but that was the long and the short of it. I could easily have stayed in Europe, and the US authorities would never have located me, nor would it have been worth the cost of the administrative process for them to try to have me extradited. Besides, European authorities don't relish the idea of tracking and chasing a guy around the countryside for being accused of "cheating on his expenses." That kind of thing is saved for high crime and murderers. Suffice it to say, my charges did not warrant any of the time, manpower, or red tape it would have taken for a manhunt or an extradition from Europe.

Captain Bartone

A friend introduced me to the police chief in the quaint European village I was staying in. I used to stop by his office in the morning for coffee. He loved to hear me tell my story and explain my charges back in the United States. He would laugh in disbelief when I explained how my offense was considered to be a second-degree crime, and a sentence of five to ten years in prison was not out of the question for such a crime.

With a chuckle, he would say, "Tell me your funny story again. What exactly did you do that would put you in prison for five to ten years? Cheat on your expenses?" In his very thick local accent, he used to say, "Hmm, what will I do if someone shows up looking for you? Well, after I'm finished laughing, I will personally escort their ass out of town in the back of my big black Mercedes Benz." Captain Bartone was a true realist.

I loved the uncomplicated, no-nonsense perspective of the people in Europe. If I didn't have family and loved ones in the United States, I might have just stayed there. However, the downside was steep, and I would have had to pay a huge price. I would never be able to return to the United States without being arrested and having to face charges. It just wasn't worth it. I concluded that it was time to face the music and head back to the States.

The Homecoming

Though most would think my incarceration was relatively short, it was filled with a gamut of "fun-filled adventures" from airport security to NY Central Booking to "The Boat" in the Bronx to Rikers Island to county jail to state prison to Intensive Supervision Parole. Being new to the wonderful world of incarceration, I was subject to my own naïveté and some bad decisions that ended up making my journey worse than it had to be.

And so the journey began. It was time to turn myself in. Having just gotten over one of the worst bouts of the flu I'd ever experienced, I boarded my plane, and off I went into the wild blue yonder, all the while hacking and coughing my brains out. When I touched down at JFK Airport, I was sure everything was going to be OK, just as my lawyer had told me. I couldn't wait to see my wife whom I had been away from for quite a while. I had resigned myself to the fact that I had limited time to get back to my home state, say my good-byes to everyone, and then accompany my lawyer to the county jail facility to turn myself in. Of course this sucked, but it was time to face the inevitable, and I had done the best I could to psyche myself into accepting that I was making the right decision.

Angels without Wings

On the airplane back to the States, I was sitting next to a very intriguing middle-aged black woman who, after hours of silence between us, looked over at me and began speaking. In the most sincere and eloquent way, she began to advise me on how to deal with life's uncertainties. About an hour before landing, right out of nowhere, she started telling me to be strong, not to worry, and to know that things were going to be OK. She went on to say that I shouldn't ever let anyone get the best of me and that I had to be on my guard.

I was speechless. I hadn't said a thing to her about my troubles or the reason I was returning to the United States. It was as if she was able to read my mind and knew what I was facing back home. After landing and getting off the airplane, I looked for this woman, but I never saw her again. It was surreal. Thoughts of her almost hypnotic smile and comforting voice would return to me often, as I embarked on my journey into a new world of chaos, corruption, and incarceration. The gentleness and compassion that exuded from this woman made me feel as if we were connected in some way. Not so much in a personal or intimate way, but in a human way. At the very least, I guess you could call it a kumbaya moment. Hey, remember what I said earlier about "humanity"? It comes in many sizes and shapes. Apparently, so do angels.

As I entered into the realm of apprehension and uncertainty and carried the weight of the world on my shoulders back to the United States, I was inspired to think about what a senseless world we live in. Later on my journey, I would write a song about it.

Angels without Wings, Part I

In this world of pain and strife
There are those who live and die by the knife
They never learned to play in harmony with life

Bitterness stings while freedom rings
There are those who know the pain that sorrow brings
But I still believe in angels without wings

Who's gonna listen to you when you call
Who's gonna catch you when you start to fall
Who's never gonna make you sit and wait
Who's gonna open up heaven's gate
The time has come to make your choice
Will you listen when you hear the voice of an angel without wings?

The Countdown
1:00 p.m.—Plan A

Man, was I in for a surprise. Like that saying that goes, "The best-laid plans of mice and men often go astray." When I got to customs and handed them my passport, I knew something wasn't right. The TSA agent called another guy, who called another guy, who showed up with two more, and I was escorted to the TSA screening area by all five of them. A bunch of people were in the screening area, mostly foreigners whose names were on some kind of terrorist list or had other immigration issues. They all came and went as I sat there for hours waiting to see what my fate would be.

Finally, I was told that I was "wanted" in another state for a felony offense. I informed them that I was well aware of the warrant and that's why I was returning to the United States—to turn myself in. I asked if I could call my lawyer, whom I really wanted to strangle at this point. No dice. No phone call. I thought if I could just speak to him and let him know what was happening, he might be able to do something to help me out of customs and allow me to follow through with our original plan to get home, see my family, say my good-byes, and then go to face the lions a day or so later. Well, so much for plan A.

All this time, I couldn't stop thinking about my wife. God, I missed her. She had come to pick me up and was probably waiting for me to miraculously appear through the customs gate, but that was not going to happen. It was time for plan B, which basically meant no plan at all.

I do declare, this would become the official starting point of having absolutely no control of anything in my life for the next two years, seven months, and twenty-one days.

4:20 p.m.—Plan B

First stop, the Port Authority Police: The NY Port Authority came to take me away from the TSA screening area and brought me to their holding tank located on the perimeter of JFK airport. First, I was searched and handcuffed, and then three Port Authority officers accompanied me through the airport toward the main entrance, which I found a bit odd. Shouldn't there be a special back exit for alleged criminals, terrorists, and lowlifes? Anyway, everyone got out of our way. It was like the parting of the Red Sea. I've been late for flights and wished everyone would get the hell out of my way like that. It's amazing how freaked out people get when they see a guy in handcuffs coming toward them. Yeah, I can laugh about it now—not so funny at the time.

When we arrived, I was placed in a cell with some Rastafarian-looking cab driver who had been arrested on some reckless endangerment charge. He wanted me to know he didn't do it and would not stop talking about it for the next four hours. I wanted to stick a rag in his mouth to shut him up, but I was feeling too damned sick and exhausted to do anything but close my eyes and try my best to tune him out. At some point, I started shivering with chills, and I was choking and coughing so hard that an officer showed up and asked if I needed medical attention. At first I said no, thinking about what implications "medical attention" might have. After a while, it got so bad that I called him back and told him I'd take him up on his offer.

Later on in my journey, I would come to realize how amazing it really was to have an officer pay attention or "give a shit" and try to help a coughing detainee. Above all, I would come to realize the difference in attitudes among jail guards. Yes, there are the good, the bad, and the downright ugly.

9:35 p.m.—Jamaica Hospital Medical Center

So, on my first night of incarceration, I was taken to the hospital for the severe coughing and breathing problems I was having. There were a lot of "firsts" that night: my first time in handcuffs (more or less), my first time in a jail cell, and now my first time in an ambulance. I was accompanied by two officers, who took me into the hospital, found me a gurney to lie on, and promptly handcuffed me to it. It was just a typical action-packed Friday night in the Jamaica Hospital emergency room: stabbings, shootings, accidents—and me, rolled out into an infirmary area and placed in the midst of about twenty other patients in beds and wheelchairs around me. It was complete chaos, but it was a lot more interesting than a jail cell.

As I lay there with an IV in my arm for dehydration and a nebulizer to help me breathe, I realized I had been placed next to another guy who was also cuffed to his bed. He was a young black guy, probably in his thirties. After a minute or so, he looked over at me, saw my cuffs, and said, "Who the fuck are you, Tony Soprano?" Being a fairly well-dressed, fifty-two-year-old, obviously Italian guy in handcuffs, I suppose that was as good a guess as any. We talked about where we were headed, and he gave me some of his best advice about how to "do" prison. The thing that really stuck in my head was when he said, "Do your time; don't let it do you." I thought that sounded pretty cool, although at that point in my journey, I had no clue what it really meant.

Most importantly, he told me there were three ways to play the game. One was to tell them you're an addict and spend your time doing methadone in the rehab unit. Two was to convince them you're crazy or that you're feeling suicidal and spend your time chilling in the mental observation unit. Three was to just jump into population and take your chances. He said that option two always worked best for him, and he highly recommended it.

I was captivated by this guy, and I was sorry I didn't catch his name or have a chance to talk a little more. As he was being rolled away by two police officers, he was announcing to everyone he passed, "Tony Soprano is in the building. That's Tony Soprano right there! That's my man, Tony!"

6:10 a.m.—Central Booking

At about 5:00 a.m., I was declared healthy enough to be released from the hospital and was taken to NY Central Booking. This is where things started getting real shitty, real fast. It was a cluster fuck of detainees, cops, and stink. It smelled like boiled eggs and urinals. This is where the Port Authority police handed me off to the NY police, who booked me. They took my passport, wallet, keys, money, and my mug shot. I wouldn't see any of my belongings again until my release. Oddly enough, for whatever reason, my things didn't remain there at Central Booking; they ended up scattered among a number of facilities and courthouses in and around New York City. Later, my wife had to embark on a ridiculous escapade that spanned multiple days as she tried to retrieve my belongings from a dozen different locations in and around Queens, New York. My wallet, passport, glasses, carry-on bag, and luggage were all at different locations.

7:35 a.m.—A Bloody Wrist with a Twist

First stop: a large cell with about twenty other guys, all of us handcuffed and sitting on the metal benches around the perimeter walls and waiting for hours for our names to be called. It never occurred to me how difficult it could be to sit upright with your hands cuffed behind your back, especially when your cuffs are tightened to the point that your wrists are beginning to show signs of blood through the raw skin.

When I complained to one of the guards, he reached behind me, spitefully twisted the handcuff chain around, and said, "There you go. Is that any better?"

"Asshole," I whispered under my breath as he started walking away.

"What the fuck did you say?" he said as he turned around and marched back toward me. Lucky for me, another guard called him out of the cell, and it pretty much ended there.

11:20 a.m.—Sandwich Hockey

Hours later, my name was called, and I was escorted to my second stop: a small cell, about sixteen feet square. They shoved twenty-one of us into this fucking cell. I counted. There was absolutely no room to move, bend, or sit, not even the floor—the literal definition of standing-room only. Ironically, the cell next to ours had no one in it. The guard came by and tossed a bunch of bologna sandwiches and cartons of milk into the cell, but nobody could reach down to pick them up without sticking their face in someone else's ass. Instead, the guys up front scooted the sandwiches and milk with their feet across the floor to the rest of us in the back of the cell.

One of the guards thought this was really funny and called another guard to watch the excellent game of sandwich hockey going on in our cell. This guy was a real asshole. I noticed his name badge because he had it on upside down. We'll just call him dickhead. I was about to collapse from lack of sleep and could barely remain on my feet at this point, but there was just no way to lie down. I managed to last another two miserable hours before some of us were escorted to our next destination.

1:40 p.m.—Pay-Phone Envy

Third stop: another cell, only smaller, and now there were only about ten of us in the cell. There was a pay phone on the wall. What a beautiful sight! I had a burning desire to talk to my wife, my kids, my lawyer—anyone in the outside world—but I wasn't the only one with this aspiration. Three guys were ahead of me. First guy, second guy, and third guy…and by the time it was my turn, it was too late because I was being dragged down the hall to my next destination. I never even got to touch that stinking phone.

2:30 p.m.—Shattered Hopes

This would be cell number four. It was another cell with a pay phone, and I latched onto it as soon as I was escorted in! I was in a minor frenzy as I grabbed the receiver and got ready to try to make a collect call. Damn it! The fucking phone was dead! I sat there dazed and staring into space until I was awakened by some kid being dragged into the cell who was literally kicking, screaming, and crying—all in a thick Latino accent.

The guys in the cell gave him about two minutes before they told him to "shut the fuck up," and one of them flung him against the wall where I was sitting. He slid down the wall slowly and sat next to me—no longer crying. He was a Puerto Rican kid named Alfonso. It turns out he was arrested for hitting his father over the head with a baseball bat. He proceeded to tell me the whole miserable story.

After checking the pay phone a half dozen times more, hoping for a miracle, I guess, I was escorted to my next destination by the "sandwich hockey" guard, pushing and shoving me all the way down the hall. Yeah, he was a real dickhead, tried and true.

Grand Slam

I first met Alfonso at NY Central Booking and then again at "The Boat," which we'll talk about later. He was a twenty-one-year-old Puerto Rican kid who lived with his parents and younger sister in Queens. He had an abusive father who had been beating his mother for as long as he could remember. Alfonso admitted that he was always afraid of his father, who was much bigger and stronger than he was. He said he had tried so many times to protect his mother from his father, but he would end up getting beaten worse than his mom.

Alfonso worked nights in the kitchen of a local restaurant. One night, he got home from work to find his mother on the living-room floor, bloody and beaten, and this time, his eighteen-year-old sister, Elena, was also a victim of his father's abuse. He heard whimpering and crying from the back of the house and found her barricaded in the bathroom. When Elena finally opened the door, Alfonso saw that she had been beaten badly. She had apparently stepped in and was trying to stop their father from beating their mom to death. She told Alfonso that their father finally stopped his rampage and passed out upstairs in his bed.

Alfonso just snapped. He went into the garage and grabbed his baseball bat and headed for his father's room. His father was lying there, sound asleep. Alfonso said he hesitated for a minute, while the years of his father's abuse and his mother's crying flashed through his mind. Then he began hitting his father over the head with the bat. He got in only about five or six blows when a police officer grabbed him from behind and tackled him to the floor. Elena had apparently called the police as soon as she saw Alfonso in the garage looking for the baseball bat. He was arrested and hauled in.

Now, here comes the ironic part. As the police were walking him out of his house to take him to the police station, he called out for his sister, Elena, and said, "Tell them! Tell them what he did to you and how he beats our mother!" She just stared back at him repulsively and said nothing. All the while, his mother was yelling at him and asking how he could be so cruel and heartless to his own father. "You are not my son. You are an animal!" she screamed at him in Spanish as they hauled him away. Wow.

As Alfonso was just finishing his story, an officer came to our jail cell to tell him his father was put on life-support in the hospital. That meant he'd likely be facing a first-degree murder charge.

4:50 p.m.—Three Bad Decisions away from Rikers

OK, cell number five. A large cell with about twenty-five guys in it. It took me a while to figure out, but this was the "holding tank" I would wait in until I was taken into the courtroom, where my short-term fate would be decided.

I was so exhausted at this point that I collapsed on the concrete floor and was able to doze off for the next few hours. I woke up when my name was called, and to my surprise, I was taken to a small cubicle to sit with a public defender (PD) and prep for my soon-to-be appearance before the judge. I explained my situation to the PD and how I had returned to the United States to turn myself in, as advised by my lawyer, and that something went wrong, blah-blah-blah, so on and so on.

The PD listened for a minute, then stopped me and said, "Look, do you want bail or not? I don't care who you are, what you did, or what went wrong. I can ask the judge for bail, and you'll probably get it. So spit it out. What's it going to be?" Here's where I made a big, big mistake. I told the PD to tell the judge that I was there to turn myself in and was not asking for bail. Within five minutes, we were in and out of the courtroom, and it was done. The PD was gone, and so was any chance of changing my mind or being able to step out of the nightmare I was embroiled in. I'd completely lost any chance to take a breather for five lousy minutes, see my wife, say good-bye, and turn myself in under halfway decent conditions.

Remember plan A? I don't think I was asking too much, which basically boiled down to a whopping forty-eight more hours of freedom. I hadn't realized the window of opportunity before me, and I let it slip away, still clinging to the idea that this whole fiasco was some kind of mistake. I thought that playing the righteous role of some poor guy who was just trying to do the right thing would somehow benefit me. Wouldn't you think?

This decision was the most naïve, ridiculous, stupid fucking thing I could have done. You see, at this point I still believed in the system, and the process, and the "justice for all" bullshit. It would take me the next few weeks of incarceration to make me truly understand what a mistake I had made. At this early point in my journey, bail might have been a perfect opportunity I had missed because I hadn't yet learned that our justice system doesn't really give a shit about the righteous, cooperative guy. That's just a fucking myth. The bottom line is that the system extends absolutely zero consideration for helping the good guy. It is completely focused on slamming the bad guy.

7:45 p.m.—Vernon C. Bain Correctional Facility (aka the Boat)

My inexperience now set the wheels into motion for being sent on an action-packed journey to Rikers Island, and that's where I was destined to remain until I could be extradited to my home state and eventually held for trial. You see, once you tell the court that you can't, or do not want to bail out, they simply start looking for a place to dump you until further notice. Not a minute wasted. You've become just another widget on the cold, steel assembly line of "justice." On the positive side, I suppose you could commend this process for being so efficient, like a well-oiled machine. On the negative side, this "assembly line" approach is the crux of the problem because it increases the potential for compromising the integrity of our penal system.

In any case, one swift kick in the ass, and you'll be on your way to whatever hellhole they have available. For me, it was the infamous Rikers Island—but wait. First, there would be one more stop in the great Empire State, and that would be The Boat, located on the Bronx side of the East River.

The Jackhammer Express

The bus ride to The Boat was a real joy. About thirty of us were handcuffed to each other as we made our way to an old, white prison transport bus. Guards shouting and chains clanging, we shuffled our way onto the bus. Still cuffed together, we all slid onto those luxurious, unpadded, solid steel bench seats and bounced our way through the streets and highways of Queens County on our way toward the Bronx. Just for fun, they must have purposely removed all shock absorbers and suspension from this fucking bus.

Between the steel seats and the "no suspension," I swear I felt every bump, thump, and pebble booting me in the ass like a jackhammer. Everyone tried to look cool and act as if they didn't notice that we were being thrown a foot in the air every time we hit a pothole in the road, but there was just no ignoring the contusions forming on my ass.

We arrived. Still cuffed to one another, we got off the bus and were directed to walk single file toward The Boat. The combination of the thrashing from our ride on the jackhammer express and being handcuffed together probably made us look like a chain gang of uncoordinated morons on their way to a slumber party. I realized then and there that the word "dignity" had just become a thing of the past for me.

11:25 p.m.—Two Bad Decisions away from Rikers

After four hours of being shuffled around in a game of "musical jail cells," we were taken to the medical intake area and spent a few more hours getting poked and prodded—or should I say, evaluated. While standing in line to have my blood taken for DNA, I heard someone shout, "Hey now, it's Tony. My man, Tony Soprano." Well, I'll be damned. It was my new pal and "advisor" from Jamaica Hospital, who, as it turns out, was nicknamed JC.

Standing next to him was Alfonso from Central Booking. Remember him, the grand-slam kid? The previous few days must have been pretty rough for Alfonso. His face looked as if he had been hit by a freight train.

A day or so had passed, and I began to realize something that never really occurred to me on the outside. I started to see that at least half of the guys I came in contact with knew each other, and even more of them had been incarcerated before, so they knew what was going to happen before it happened—especially my present company there at The Boat. Worse than that, some of these guys seemed to be having a good old time, as if we were at the annual high-school picnic or something.

There wasn't anything I could do about it, but this really bugged the shit out of me. It's hard to put into words, but when you're feeling beaten and broken and the system has just reduced you to a worthless, low-life piece of shit, it sucks to have a bunch of romper-room dickheads lapping it up like we're off to summer camp or something! I knew I had to let this frustration go or it was going to make me crazy. I would soon learn that this romper-room bullshit was only going to get worse as my journey continued forward.

Still being shuffled around the medical intake area, I was able to have a conversation with JC, this time a little more detailed than when we were chained to our beds in the hospital emergency area a few nights before.

He explained, "Now's your chance to make your move, Tony. When they bring you over to that 'psych' dude at the next line, you gotta tell 'em you be thinkin' 'bout suicide. Tell 'em you just can't make it up in here."

So that's what I did. I told the guy I was thinking about suicide. I don't know if this guy was a psychiatrist, doctor, counselor, or just some corrections idiot, but he seemed cool about it and just sent me on my way. Little did I know that the eventual outcome of this little conversation would prove to be a nightmare.

After the medical-intake crap was finished, I was placed in a shithole of a cell for the night with another fifteen guys—thirteen black guys, one Asian guy, and me. I was obviously out of my element, but not even close to how much this little Asian guy stood out. He was screaming through the bars of the cell at all the guards in Chinese, or Japanese, or whatever "nese" he was. If it wasn't for how obnoxious and ridiculously entertaining this guy was to watch, I'm sure he would have gotten a good beatdown by either the detainees or the guards. He was like some cartoon circus act on steroids, or one of those little kung fu guys zipping around like a demented ninja. Finally, the guards hauled him out of there kicking and screaming all the way down the hall. After ten minutes, you could still hear his screaming and wailing, eventually fading into the distance.

Lights-out. Everyone started trying to scope out some space on the concrete for the night. I finally found mine. I lay down and tried to sleep, but no dice. Instead of counting sheep, I begin to formulate some phrases in my head, and I was repeating them over and over again as I stared up at the ceiling; cold, steel bars; and gray cinder-block walls around me.

I memorized those phrases. As my journey through the miserable world of incarceration continued from days to weeks to months, I gradually put the words to the melody of a song written by an old friend of mine. This song stayed with me, swirling in my head and consoling me as I began traveling the long road toward redemption.

The Concrete Is My Only Friend

In this hotel of steel, scarred by the knife,
Where I fight for my sanity and I question my life,
My quest is for somewhere to lay down my head,
Surrounded by concrete, no refuge, no bed...

I've been through hell and back again; the concrete is my only friend

And so I surrender and behold its embrace,
It's the concrete that warms me, and kisses my face,
I yearn for the peace and the calm she provides,
Knowing freedom is less than a cry from outside...

I've been through hell and back again; the concrete is my only friend

Time passes slowly with plenty to burn; I crave consolation, God help me discern
Another hour, another day, I close my eyes and fade away...and I'm free

6:30 a.m.—One Bad Decision from Rikers

Rise and shine. We were given our trays of so-called breakfast, and the action-packed day began at the infamous Boat. Guards were buzzing around everywhere, calling out names, shuffling people around, and dishing out the typical offensive bullshit that they do so well. I heard the guys in my cell talking about how great it was that they were on their way to a bed and a shower and some level of normalcy—relatively speaking, of course. But that didn't happen for me.

Eventually, everyone in my cell was called and sent off to their newly assigned tier, or wing, or who knows what. I sat there for a few hours after everyone else in my cell was gone, once again wondering what my fate might be. Finally, I was called and escorted out of my holding cell to what turned out to be a small observation cell in the intake area. OK, so now what? I sat there for a few more hours, and then I saw the psych guy I had spoken with the night before. He was pointing at me and the two guys in the observation cells next to mine and talking to the guards. Then

I overheard two of them talking, and one of them said, "These three nut cases are going to the island for observation."

What? The island? A guy from the next cell looked over at me and said, "Hey, man, have you ever been there? To Rikers Island, I mean?" Holy shit! My heart dropped. I slid down the wall to the floor and just sat there. *I'm going to Rikers Island. Holy shit, I'm going to Rikers Island?* I repeated under my breath over and over again.

"Damned right, old man, we goin' to the island, just like Bahama, Jamaica, and Hono-fuckin-lulu!" the guy in the next cell chanted like a bad rap song.

About half an hour later, the psych guy came back. He walked up to my cell and asked, "How you doing today, sir? You still having those thoughts? You thinking about killing yourself?"

I didn't respond right away, but I started to speak: "Uh, well, I don't know, but—"

He cut me off and called out to the guards, "OK, OK, guys, all three of them, then. Call me if there's a problem." And off he went.

"Hey, wait a minute, wait a minute!" I yelled out to him as he ignored me and made his way out of the intake area.

Another bad decision? Fuck, yes! It just bought me a ticket to Rikers Island, man. It had to be. I was beginning to think that my "advisor and good buddy," JC, might have been dishing out some bad advice. Either that or I was just missing something. Or maybe I just plain old sucked at this incarceration thing. If I didn't tell the psych guy I was thinking about suicide, I probably wouldn't have been going to Rikers and might have been settling into some of that "normalcy" crap the guys were talking about in my cell that morning. But that also meant I'd be heading for a bed in "population," which I had been convinced was not the place for an old, inexperienced, regular dude like me.

At this point, I was completely overwhelmed, exhausted, and confused by all of the guesswork and speculation. Out on the streets, whether it's your personal life or your business life, things aren't really that hard to figure out, and learning the ropes always came fairly easy to me. Not here, not now.

Anyway, the three of us "nut cases" were taken into the back of an office area while the guards were doing some kind of preparation and paperwork. There was a phone on the wall. Pay dirt! The elusive telephone was my only hope of a connection to the outside world and a little slice of sanity. You have no idea how such a simple pleasure as being able to make a phone call could ever mean so much to you.

One of the guys asked if he could use the phone, and to my absolute shock, the guard said something like, "You'd better make it fast, and you'd better make it collect." All three of us guys wanted to get on that phone so badly, we were ready to kill for it. These two guys, having much more experience than me on prison telephone etiquette, explained to me that you could call only a landline on this prison phone, not a cell phone.

Because only one guy had a landline call to make, he would make his call first, and when he finished, we would "piggyback" the other two calls from the landline to the cell phone numbers we wanted. What that actually meant was that the first guy's girlfriend would have to use her cell phone to make a call to our wives and then hold her cell phone up to the receiver of the landline while we spoke. As unbelievable as it sounds, it worked, and we all made our calls. Brilliant!

I was able to talk to my wife for the first time since I had left Europe several days earlier. Most importantly, I was able to tell her I loved her and that I was OK—well, basically—and that I was on my way to Rikers Island. Last but not least, I was able to tell her to let my lawyer know that he should prepare his law partner for an upcoming murder trial—his! Yes, right about then, I was so angry and frustrated that I had been thrown on this one-way freight train to hell that I was ready to strangle him for whatever blunder might have allowed this nightmare to happen.

3:15 p.m.—Welcome to Rikers Island

Prison guards. I guess it's time to start calling them by their proper title, which is CO, short for corrections officer. When I arrived at Rikers, I was placed in a holding tank with a guy who was blasted on heroin while they figured out where they were going to put me. This guy was dozing on and off and vomiting all over himself all at the same time. Cute. My exhaustion was unbearable, and I collapsed on the floor of the cell. Once again, I felt as if the concrete was my only friend.

Some asshole CO came over and started banging a nightstick on the bars of the cell. He yelled, "Hey, you'd better not be dead. You ain't gonna die on my watch, motherfucker."

I didn't move an inch. I wasn't facing him, so he couldn't see that my eyes were open and I was just lying there, alive. He started banging harder and screaming louder until I finally rolled over and looked back at him. He stopped, but another CO went over and told him to "calm the fuck down," to which he replied, "Go fuck yourself, Jack." The decent CO looked at me and asked, "You OK? You don't look so good."

"Me? I'm OK, but you might want to keep an eye on Mr. Vomit sitting in the corner" I answered with a slight smile on my face and then thanked him for asking.

I got up off the floor and happened to notice the screaming asshole CO's name badge. It was the same last name as the dickhead with the upside-down name badge at the county courthouse a few days earlier—the "sandwich hockey" prick. Wow, was there a family somewhere in Queens tasked to breed dickhead COs for the New York criminal justice system? I was really starting to despise some of these guys. There appeared to be about a four-to-one ratio of dickheads to decent COs. More about that later.

Eventually, I was escorted to the infirmary area, where I waited for what turned out to be yet another mental intake assessment. I was able to talk openly to two of the intake workers, who I believe were actual psychologists. I answered a ton of questions and told each of them about my situation. I explained how I didn't understand why I wasn't just being expedited to my home state, and I once again clarified my intention to turn myself in. I thought I was actually making some progress and that it might have some impact on getting me out of the New York system and back to my home state.

In the outside world, two reasonable, intelligent adults can have a conversation, and things will usually work out well. Think again. I guess once you open your mouth about contemplating suicide, it just can't be undone. About ten minutes after speaking with the intake workers, I was escorted away and taken to what turned out to be some kind of mental observation unit. I'm not sure of its exact purpose, but I was taken to what a few detainees were calling "the fucking hex of doom."

In my entire life, I have never experienced a more disgusting, putrid, vile place. Over the next four days, I would face the absolute worst of humanity in both the detainees and the COs.

Rikers Island—"Some Kinda Mental Isolation Unit"

The first day started with five of us in "the hex," an observation cell that was almost the shape of a halved hexagon. Outside of this cell, there was a guard station with a desk. On average, there were about two or three COs there to watch over the prisoners and the other isolation cells across from it. (You know, I get frustrated as I realize that I may not have the correct names for all of these "lovely" locations I was assigned to. It's not as if there's a tour guide hanging around to answer questions. You are left essentially clueless about the what, where, and why things are happening to you. All you know is that you're being dragged from one place to another and thrown wherever you're thrown. People have asked, "Oh, were you on this wing, or that one, or this tier, or that unit?" Honestly, I didn't fucking know *where* I was half the time—or why.)

Here's a quick rundown of the four crazy bastards residing in the hex with me:

Prisoner 1 was a psychotic kid in his early twenties named Tommy with some serious issues. When he wasn't staring at you with that Charles Manson look and threatening to "jump your ass" if you didn't give him your shoes—yep, that's right, your "shoes"—he would sit in the corner of the room peeking out the window at the female COs while jerking off with some sick look on his face. There never seemed to be anything *but* female COs guarding this unit. I have no idea why.

Prisoner 2 was some insane black guy in his late twenties. His name was Roger. Just days earlier, he had attacked and stabbed his mother to death while she was taking a shower. He loved talking about it, and he would go back and forth from giggling to crying as he described the attack and why he did it. Do you really want to know? It was her naked body's fault. It kept making him stare at her and making him hate himself and making him want to kill "it"—her body, that is.

Prisoner 3 was a guy from Montana in his thirties named Wes. He was arrested for "train hopping" his way to New York, but additional charges seemed inevitable. Tommy, the psycho kid, told me that when the cops caught him, he was in a freight car with a finger in his pocket, only it wasn't his, nor was it connected to anyone else. He claimed to have bitten it off of someone on his train ride to New York. Tommy was nuts, so who knows whether it was true or just one of Tommy's own sick fantasies.

Prisoner 4 was...Alfonso! That's right. Once again, our paths had crossed. You already know Alfonso's grand-slam story of his abusive father and a baseball bat.

And prisoner 5 was me. A white-collar-crime guy in his early fifties who, whether fortunately or unfortunately, depending on how you look at it, had convinced the "powers that be" that he was feeling miserable about the predicament he was in and had uttered that magical word, "suicide."

I began to realize just how convincing I must have been that I would end up with this gang of merry freaking marauders. Days in the hex were very, very long. We were there twenty-four hours a day. Not twenty-three hours with some kind of one-hour break. I'm talking twenty-four hours. Even being thrown in the "bing," which is a punitive isolation unit, would give you one hour of time out of your cell. For the entire four days, I was in the hex, I never left it, not even for one minute.

There was a toilet covered in shit, urine, flies, and garbage to the point that you could not use it without spending ten minutes cleaning a pathway and finding some piece of paper, cardboard, or milk carton to wipe down the seat with, or your ass, for that matter. I asked for a trash bag and a broom to clean it up myself. Practically in unison, I received a resounding "go fuck yourself" from the three female COs. I was beginning to believe those were the only three words these COs knew.

The other problem was that the toilet itself was filled with garbage, so flushing was not an option. I won't go into any further detail on this subject; I'm sure you can imagine it for yourself. For four days straight, there appeared to be no plan for cleaning or sanitizing this cell. Absolutely none. I remember thinking that there were probably prisoner-of-war camps with better conditions than this.

The only respite for me was to try to sleep. Sleeping was my escape, and for the first time in my life, I was actually trying to force myself to sleep for as many hours as my body would allow in a twenty four hour period. With thoughts of my "angel without wings" and that song I composed at

NY Central Booking, "The Concrete Is My Only Friend" constantly playing in my head, I managed to stake claim to a piece of floor space just big enough to lie down on, and I defended it with my life. By the second night in the hex, I had already had two brawls doing so. Oh, in case you are wondering, the COs would just watch these fights and do absolutely nothing about them—except maybe laugh a little.

Then all hell broke loose. Two new guys were brought in, so now there were seven of us in the hex. I never caught their names. These two guys weren't just crazy; they were ultraviolent assholes. They intimidated everyone in the cell by kicking and slugging them on a whim. They were stealing everyone's food. Even though the food was about the worst slop you could possibly imagine, it was all we had. To have it taken away really sucked. One of them even pissed on Wes's face, the guy from Montana, while he was sleeping on the floor. They had everyone in the cell scared to even breathe. They were especially hard on Alfonso, throwing him around like a basketball half the time and the rest of the time twisting his arms behind his back to the point that he could hardly move them anymore.

I could not believe where I was and what was happening around me. It was beyond comprehension. Nothing in the human experience could have prepared me for the chaos, insanity, and injustice I was fucking submerged in. I had heard of Rikers Island and its horrible reputation but could never have imagined there was a place as vile as this on American soil.

To realize the irony and the senselessness of the situation, remember that I was still just a detainee at this point, meaning that I hadn't even been tried or convicted of anything. You can cackle all you want and spew out that typical "He's a convicted criminal; what the hell does he expect?" bullshit, but at this point, when you're still a detainee and you haven't been tried, it has yet to be determined whether you are even guilty of anything. You could be an innocent man just waiting to be tried. Does being kept in these conditions sound like justice for all? No fucking way.

A Rude Awakening

It was my third night in the hex. Better yet, seventy-two hours of prison-style isolation. It had to be hotter than a hundred degrees in that cell, and at times, it actually became hard to breathe. If we asked the COs to please do something about the heat, we were completely ignored. As outrageous as it sounds, I think they really enjoyed watching us suffer. It was just a disgusting, stinking shithole of a place to be—kind of like a porta-potty on a hot and sticky summer day.

Sometime in the middle of the night, I was awakened by yelling and screaming and someone grabbing my arm. It was Alfonso. He was being beaten by Tommy and the two new guys. I looked out the window at the two female COs and yelled for help. They actually got up off their fat asses to watch the assault from outside of the window of the hex but were doing nothing about it—just watching!

I was only a few feet away from the beating, and I couldn't stand it any longer. I was sure they were going to kill him. I jumped in and tried to stop them. I tried to pull them off Alfonso, but one of them kicked me in the head and knocked me half-senseless across the room. As I crawled back toward the beating, I saw Tommy stick a plastic spoon into Alfonso's eye. It stood straight up, wedged in his eye socket.

At that point, they stopped beating him as Alfonso just lay there convulsing and groaning. I was able to crawl back to Alfonso and pull the plastic spoon out of his eye. I sat in the corner, holding his head on my lap for what seemed like an eternity before three male COs finally showed up, stormed in the door, and hauled Alfonso away, presumably to the hospital. The female COs suddenly acted like they gave a shit as they ran into the hex right after the male COs and pretended to help.

I still have nightmares and relive that vile attack on Alfonso. I am still haunted by the sickening grin on the female COs' faces as they watched him get beaten half to death. I was over fifty years old, and I had never felt such rage. For the first time in my life, I knew how it felt to actually want to kill someone. I will always despise those COs for introducing me to such a repulsive feeling, and God forgive me for the horrific things I wished upon them for allowing this unforgivable brutality to happen to that poor kid, Alfonso.

The Temper-Mental Ward

After four days of complete hell, I was released from this "hex of doom" and sent to my next destination, which was a cell located in a tier full of guys with various mental issues. I would remain there until my eventual Queen's County Court date and extradition to county jail in my home state. Well, almost. Yeah, this time I was kind-of-sort-of able to identify where I landed.

That's because, for the first time since I'd been at Rikers, the CO who escorted me out of the hex struck up a conversation with me about it being his first week on the job. He was very talkative and seemed like a decent guy. I was walking alongside him and feeling absolutely fantastic about being out of a cell full of psychos and actually walking and moving around like a normal human being.

Then I made the mistake of following my CO escort into the center of the hallway. That was a bad thing to do. At Rikers, when you're being escorted down the halls, detainees are required to walk on the outer perimeter of the hall behind a painted boundary on the floor. No one told me this, including my new CO escort! Only guards and staff are allowed in the center of the hallway. All hell broke loose.

Two COs came up to us, screaming at both me and the new CO, and proceeded to shove me across the hallway and up against the wall. I hit my head against the wall so hard that I lost my hearing and my balance for a minute, compounded by the fact that I had just been kicked in the head a few nights earlier. Both the new CO and I were verbally blasted for five minutes straight. My friendly, talkative, "decent" CO escort changed his tune entirely and never looked at me or said another word to me.

I was taken to my cell. It was absolute heaven! One, I was by myself. Two, I had a metal-framed bed with a two-inch, so-called mattress. Three, I had a toilet without shit, piled-up garbage, and a year's worth of stink and filth around it. Four, there was a gray wool blanket and a two-inch foam pillow—the crappiest ones you can imagine, but I was thrilled nonetheless. Five, there was an actual shower down the hall. And six, there were two pay phones on the wall. Pay dirt! It's amazing how your standards can be reduced to the lowest of low after a week in that Rikers POW-style mental-observation cell I was in.

For the next week or so, I actually settled into a decent frame of mind. Having my own six-by-ten-foot cell and a chance to leave it once in a while was absolutely liberating. Access to a shower and a telephone was like paradise. I even had a small window in my cell. If you focused real hard past the weeds and about five layers of various barbed wire and chain-link fences, you could almost see the long bridge that leads to Rikers Island. Well, whaddaya know…a room with a view.

There's not much to do, but you make the best of it. Everyone latches onto anything they can just to stay sane, notwithstanding the fact that everyone in this unit was supposed to be some kind of crazy. Some guys read books, some played games, some watched TV in the lunchroom, some prayed all day to Allah, and some waited obsessively for medication time.

Meds were handed out through a small portal in the bars at the entrance of the unit. You were given one little paper cup with your meds and another with water to take them in front of the nurse or tech who was handing them to you. It was difficult to hoard medication, but some guys were able to "mouth" their pills without getting caught and then save them to trade or take later in multiple doses. I'm talking about those detainees who were on medications of recreational value, of course. These guys would trade their meds for whatever they could get—stuff like tomorrow's lunch, food from your commissary, soap, toothpaste, socks, or whatever you can imagine.

Later on in my journey, I would learn that at Rikers, it was actually easier to get away with "mouthing" medications than it would be in county jail or state prison. Though heroin and coke were obtainable, the most common recreational meds available were the benzodiazepine derivatives *such as Ativan, Valium, and Xanax. As you would expect, these were the meds that were most frequently prescribed to detainees because they are for sleep issues, depression, and anxiety. Everyone talked and dreamed about getting some OxyContin, Percocet, or Vicodin, but for obvious reasons, they are seldom prescribed to detainees. They were like gold if you could get them.*

Keister Sunday Cookies

A new guy named Davie came to the unit with a huge stash of pills. No one knew how or where he got all these medications, but he quickly became the "go-to guy for a cheap high."

After days of wheeling and dealing his pills, everyone was getting more and more curious about where he was getting them and how he was sneaking them into the unit. The assumption was that he was mouthing them because the pills looked a bit worn and dampened. At first, he refused to tell anyone how he was doing it, but he eventually spilled the beans and told someone that his girlfriend was a CO and that she was supplying him. That satisfied everyone's curiosity for a day or so, but then someone said, "Hey, wait a minute, there *is* no female CO on our unit. How the hell does he get them in here?"

The next morning at breakfast, I could tell something weird was going on. No one was talking, everyone seemed weird, and Davie was at a table all by himself. This was something you never saw because he was usually the most popular kid on the block, if you know what I mean. All of a sudden, about five guys jumped up and started pounding on Davie. The COs were there within a minute and quickly dragged him to his cell. I sat there shocked and asked my buddy, Dick, what the hell was going on. He said that Davie finally told someone how he was getting the meds in. He was sticking them up his ass.

As the story goes, his CO girlfriend would take the medication to him when he attended his AA meetings. There, he was able to shove them up his ass until he got back to the unit. OK, no big deal. The human ass has long been a vehicle for drug smuggling, and no one in prison has much of a problem with that. But here's the clincher: Davie shoved them directly up his ass—no plastic bag, no balloon, no nothing! That didn't fly with the guys. Two curious detainees witnessed him digging the pills directly out of his ass! Yep, he would just "dig" them out, wipe them off, and start wheeling and dealing away.

Uh-oh—this is an example of some very bad "ass etiquette." As you might imagine, the "Keister Sunday Cookies" routine did not sit well with all the guys who had the pleasure of swallowing his slightly damp, superficially stained pills. That night, four guys delivered another righteous beating to Davie in the shower area. This time, the COs removed him from the tier.

Corrections Officers: The Good, the Bad, and the Ugly

You quickly learn how important it is to scope out the COs and determine which ones are reasonable and which ones are complete assholes. You learn which COs to fear and which ones actually give a damn and try to do the right thing. As I mentioned earlier, the ratio between the two is not always reassuring. At Rikers, COs are a rare breed. When I consider my entire journey through incarceration, I encountered both the worst and best COs at Rikers.

Some of them seemed as if they just wanted to get the job done and go home, like most everyone else in the free world. They were fair and reasonable and would actually treat you like a human being most of the time. Others were sick bastards. I'm talking about out-and-out heartless and evil in some cases. Believe me, I surprise myself every time I read my own words, but some of these fucked-up egotistical bastards actually got off on watching people suffer.

I was involved in an incident in which three of us guys were taken to an isolated cell and forced to strip naked and get beaten by two male and two female COs using a nightstick with a towel wrapped around it. Why the towel? So there would be no bruising. Why the beating? Because one of the guys complimented a female CO on how good-looking she was.

The third guy and I just happened to be sitting next to him when he said it—a classic case of being at the wrong place at the right time. That infamous day, I received a deep laceration on my inner thigh. Yes, I was scarred by the dull knife of one of the COs who held it against my leg, threatening to cut me in a certain place if I didn't stay quiet. That scar serves as a constant reminder of that brutal event. But what's worse is the scar on my psyche coming back to haunt me at the oddest times and places.

There is a lot more I could say about this particular incident, but I won't. Let's just say that if my subsequent post-traumatic stress issues didn't deter me, this incident would have made for a good lawsuit after I left prison. And there were other incidents. Like the time when one of those same COs ordered three asshole detainees into the cell of some guy who had pissed him off and ordered the detainees to beat the guy half to death during lockdown. Come on, people, if this stuff doesn't substantiate the fact that things are a little out of control, then what the hell does? I'll remind you once again that most of us hadn't been to trial and could have been completely innocent at this point in time.

Although some COs were fair, reasonable, and at times even somewhat compassionate, there was a glaring, systemic flaw that canceled out any good that might come from them: complacency! Although some of these guys did not partake in the abuses of the unjust and often repulsive actions of their fellow COs, they did nothing to stop those who did, nor did it appear that they reported them to anyone of authority or consequence. Ever hear the phrase "Apathy breeds corruption and incompetence"? Damn fucking right it does.

I will surely piss off a lot of people for saying this, but our current system for choosing qualified corrections officer candidates and providing them with proper, as well as effective training, must be pathetic. There must be a whole lot of focus on the use of intimidation, force, handcuffs, leg irons, batons, and Tasers and very little on rational thinking, stress management, problem solving, and, dare I say it, rehabilitation. What's worse is that our prison culture has become so demoralized and anesthetized to its own deficiencies that digging out of the downward spiral we're in would require more time, effort, and money than anyone appears to have the stomach for.

Remember, I am someone who has been behind those bars and has witnessed and experienced the abusive nature of our prison system firsthand, so I will end this section with one simple thought: yes, apathy does breed corruption and incompetence. Shouldn't the most powerful, democratic country in the world (and incidentally, the one with the highest per-capita incarceration rate of all nations) hold itself to the highest possible standards when it comes to justice, morality, and the reparation of our penal system? Shouldn't an incarcerated American citizen receive better treatment than a terrorist at Guantanamo Bay? Well, it appears that they often don't. Call me biased or call me crazy, but I answer an emphatic yes to both questions.

The Ballad of Dick and Jane

Dick was a young guy I met while in the mental tier. He was sure he knew me and came running up to me as I was taken to my cell. He thought I was the owner of the pizza place near his mom's house in the Bronx. He was so amped up about seeing me that I didn't have the heart to tell him I wasn't the guy he thought I was, so I just went with it. Whenever we were out of our cells, for meals, meds, or whatever, he would find me and start talking about the old neighborhood and all the good times he had at my pizza joint. He had everyone calling me "pizza man."

And then there was Jane. He was a spirited gay man who gallantly walked the walk and talked the talk. While the tier was locked down and everyone was in their cells, Jane would come a callin'. He apparently had the cooperation of the COs because it was like clockwork—same time every night after dinner, he would poke his head into the small window on the door of your cell with his makeup and bright red lipstick, fluttering his eyes and blowing kisses in hopes of getting an invitation. I'm not really sure what kind of price was attached to the proposition, or even if there was one.

One day, shortly after Jane had already passed my cell and was making his rounds, I heard screaming and hollering coming from somewhere down the hall. It sounded as if someone was being killed. It lasted about five minutes and then was over. I didn't find out until the next day, when I realized that Dick was gone, that he and Jane had a lover's spat. Holy shit! I didn't even know Dick was gay, let alone in love with Jane.

As the story goes, Dick wanted Jane to himself and had asked Jane to stop making the rounds with guys on the tier. That didn't happen. So when Dick and Jane got together that night, the sparks were flying. During their encounter, Dick bit Jane's penis hard enough to bleed profusely. The COs quickly took them both away, and, of course, I never saw either of them again.

The next day, there was still blood on the floor of the cell, around the doorway, and into the hall. I remember it all too well, as I, mister "pizza man," was one of the guys chosen to help clean it up.

Farewell to Rikers Island

The day finally came. My name was called, and I was escorted to a small room where I was once again interviewed by a psychologist. Yes, this time I asked exactly who the hell he was and actually got a polite answer: "I am a shrink...and a civilian employee of this facility." Wow, it was always refreshing to hear a polite and cohesive sentence that didn't include "go fuck yourself" or "shut the fuck up" or "motherfucker."

He asked the same old questions, including the most relevant and popular one: "Do you still feel like killing yourself?" I was more careful about how I answered him than I had ever been in previous interviews. My answer, in essence, was no. As I mentioned earlier, I had learned that there was a fine line that must not be crossed when answering this volatile question, for fear that you might be thrown directly into some kind of hellhole—or who knows where. I did my best to walk that proverbial fine line and prayed I would stay in my newfound, plain old, relatively bearable, so-called mental tier.

The psychologist left, and I was taken back to my cell. I thought everything had gone well and that I had finally provided a response that would keep me from being dragged back to the evil observation hex of doom. In spite of this, that night my name was called, and I was ordered to pack up my things because I was being relocated. What things? All I had were the clothes on my back, a second pair of underwear, and a toothbrush. So where was I going now?

As my CO escort and I proceeded down the halls of Rikers, I felt sickened by the thought that they might be bringing me back to the stinking hellhole, but I soon realized we were in new territory, a part of Rikers I'd never seen before. I started thinking that maybe I was finally on my way out of the whole fucking nightmare, and my heart started pounding at the mere thought of finally leaving Rikers.

Then we arrived. Oh, no. It didn't take me long to figure this one out. I'd been brought to "suicide watch."

"Oh, boy, this is going to be fucking fun," I said under my breath.

The CO heard me, chuckled a little, and said, "Ain't no worse than the looney bin they had you in for four days straight."

I had my doubts about that as I was made to strip naked and put on a sleeveless garment called a "suicide smock." That's because it is too bulky to make into a noose and too tough to tear, rendering it essentially useless for killing yourself.

Once again, two female COs were watching this unit. It was starting to occur to me that the more humiliating the unit, like the observation hex, or suicide watch, or the bing, the more they tended to have female COs assigned to it.

Think about it. In suicide watch, you're bare-ass naked wearing a ridiculous smock with your "junk" hanging out. You're supposedly crazy as all fuck and more likely to flip out on a whim than everybody else. You probably stink from not having access to a daily shower. And some genius official decides, "Hey, now, what a great place to stick all the female COs."

Are they morons or just plain assholes? You decide. At any rate, what the fuck was this all about? What was the logic? Not that I wanted to go there, but why was I taken here instead of the nightmarish "hex" I was in before? Nothing seemed to make any sense. It didn't take long to figure out that this was actually a few notches better than the hex.

I must reiterate how the thought process and logic of the "powers that be" never ceased to amaze and confuse the hell out of me. Like I said before, they don't tell you jack shit about what's going on, so I didn't know that I would be leaving in the morning to go to the Queens County Courthouse for my extradition hearing and would never see the likes of Rikers again. Did this have something to do with the reason they decided to put me into suicide watch then—on my last night at Rikers? Who the fuck knows?

It was pitch black in that cell. All I could really see was the shadow around the cell door and a faint light from an obscured observation window. It was creepy, but very peaceful. No fighting for a space on the concrete floor. No psycho assholes there to harass you, beat you, or stick spoons in your eyes. Not bad at all.

The next morning, at about 5:00 a.m. came the big surprise. I was awakened by pounding on the cell door. A female CO walked into the cell as I was lying there with my balls hanging in the breeze and tossed me what I thought were my clothes.

"Get dressed, pizza man. I'm coming back for you in five minutes. You hear me, pizza man? You're going to court today," she said. Fan-fucking-tastic! Those were the best words I had heard in weeks!

To my surprise, what she had handed me was a gray jumpsuit. I soon learned that these were given to the supposed "nut cases" like me, to distinguish us from the normal detainees. A few of us jumpsuit nut cases were lined up in the hallway waiting to be escorted. Soon we were on our way, and we began the trek down the halls of Rikers to the transportation area. Wow, I was amazed by the number of detainees being shuffled in and out and around the transport area—just a massive amount of activity. All I can think of to compare it to is Grand Central Station. It's mind-boggling that they are able to get a thousand guys to their destinations every day like clockwork. I was frazzled but also quite impressed.

Another thing I was impressed with was the CO in charge. I think he was a lieutenant. He "did me a solid," a new phrase I learned from the guy behind me in line. After miraculously managing to get his attention, I pleaded with him and told him that I was some kind of government official, that I was probably going to get photographed by the paparazzi, and that I really didn't want to be in a gray jumpsuit when I left the courtroom. He left, came back with my paper bag of street clothes, and said, "You've got one minute to put these on and get your ass on that bus."

Soon I was outbound, crossing the infamous Rikers Island bridge and looking back behind me at the huge, gray, blatantly cold, and emotionless hotel of steel called Rikers Island. I could hardly believe I was really on my way to Queens County court. As crazy as it sounds, I couldn't wipe the smile off my face, feeling like things could only get better from here.

The Legend of Battery Swallow

During my fabulous night in suicide watch, I encountered this shithead gangbanger who had swallowed a bunch of batteries that he somehow got a hold of while he was working in the kitchen. This guy claimed that he was being targeted and that his life was in danger, and he asked to be transferred from his tier but was denied. He succeeded in getting moved from his tier, but things didn't go quite as he expected, and he landed in suicide watch. In desperation, he decided to try the old battery swallow trick.

In case you were wondering, swallowing nine AA's is not a very intelligent idea. The best-case scenario was that he would simply pass the batteries with or without a potentially agonizing toilet experience before they had a chance to do any major harm. The worst-case scenario was that he would suffer from a bowel obstruction or the acid from the batteries would begin to break down in his stomach, burn his insides, and potentially kill him. In the meantime, he would remain under surveillance in suicide watch.

It was in the middle of the night when the screaming began. I swear, this guy was screaming in agony for help for an hour before anyone even showed up to see what the fuck was going on. When they finally showed up, he was pulled from his cell and laid down on the floor outside my cell. I sat on the floor with my ear pressed against the door of my cell so I could hear but not see what was going on.

This guy was screaming at the top of his lungs in pain, and the guards, about three of them, were screaming back at him to "shut the fuck up!" This screaming back and forth went on for about ten minutes straight and then suddenly ended...in silence. The guy was eventually shuffled away, so I don't know exactly what happened to him. I don't know whether the batteries burst inside of him or if he developed a bowel obstruction. Did he die? Who knows?

After a while, things calmed down outside my cell. I sat there on the floor of my dark, suicide-watch cell with my head still pressed against the door—naked, cold, and shaking. I heard one CO say to another, "What the fuck is wrong with you? You didn't have to beat the piss out of him like that. If this one bites the dust, it's on you."

Queens County Courthouse

I slept almost all the way to the courthouse. Unlike the last ride I had taken on the Rikers express, this bus actually seemed to have some genuine shock absorbers. That, plus my level of exhaustion, made it pretty easy to fall asleep. We arrived at the courthouse and were promptly herded into the back entrance. Once again, it was time for the roundup at the OK Corral. Like livestock, we were prodded, hollered at, and driven into our corrals. Yippee kai yay! I guess I will never get over the cowboy round-'em-up sensation I would experience every time we were transported into and out of a facility. Git along, little freakin' doggies.

My cell was clean and looked freshly painted in shitty shades of gray-on-gray and tarnished steel, but it was clean. I immediately claimed some real estate on the cool concrete floor. Ahh, my best friend. I dozed off and on for hours as multiple groups of detainees came in and were called out of the cell. It was about three or four in the afternoon when my name was called. I was the last person in the cell. Two guards escorted me down the halls and into the courtroom. There was a female judge who had an attitude not too different than Judge Judy you see on TV. I liked her, and I'll tell you why. A public defender and the two officers from my home state who had come to extradite me back home were standing alongside me, facing the judge.

The judge asked me, "Are you aware that you are being extradited? Do you have any objections or anything you would like to say to this court?" Before I could even open my mouth, the two officers jumped up and started babbling about their orders and waving around some document.

"Shut your mouths!" she screamed at them and pounded her fist. "I am addressing the detainee, not you! Now, you will remain silent until you are directly addressed by this court. Do you understand?" the judge said.

Wow, this was great. I loved it. It was the first tiny piece of respect I'd received in a long time. Instead of having to struggle to get someone to listen to me, the judge actually encouraged me to explain who I was and the details of my circumstances. She was stern but polite, and I found her attitude extremely refreshing after what I'd been through on my Rikers Island journey. She actually smiled at me and wished me the best of luck as I was led out of the courtroom by my two new buddies.

These two officers actually turned out to be pretty decent. They let me wear my handcuffs in front instead of behind my back as we made the long trek home. They had a hundred questions for me about Rikers. They seemed fascinated to meet someone who had actually been there and amazed by what I was describing to them. It made the ride relatively pleasant—all things considered, of course. I even laughed for the first time in a long while.

I know it's hard to believe, but at that moment in time, I actually felt good. I guess liberated would be more accurate. Rikers Island had been such a cluster fuck and a nightmare that after just twelve hours away from it, I began to feel rejuvenated.

CHAPTER 3
The Grand Entrance

County Jail

So, there I was. Finally made it home and into the County Detention Center, better known as jail. This is where I would live for the next six months, where my life would continue to be put on hold, where our criminal justice system would decide my fate, and where I would eventually be sentenced to state prison.

As we entered the county facility, three people were waiting for our arrival. The prosecutor, who was behind glass in a guard booth of some sort, was peering out at me as if they were bringing in some high-profile crime boss. The other two were the county sheriff and some old CO sergeant who looked like Wyatt Earp.

Wow, they were really proud of themselves, as if there had been a massive manhunt with blazing bullets, sirens, swat teams, and bullhorns! Yeah, right. It felt more like an old episode of "Dragnet." It was borderline embarrassing. The whole time, I kept thinking, *Uhh, hello! I turned myself in, assholes! You did nothing. I'd still be sipping French wine in Paris for all you did to capture me!*

Anyway, the sheriff started ragging on and on about how I was going to get eighty-eight years for all the redundant charges they had piled up against me. One of the officer escorts was standing behind the sheriff practically rolling his eyes and smirking at him as he ranted and performed his mister macho routine, confirming what I already knew, which was that the big, bad sheriff was talking out of his ass.

The whole while, I just stood there with a half-smile on my face. So naturally, they piled it on thicker and thicker, trying to get a rise out of me.

"Stand over here, boy. Get against the wall, detainee, hands behind your head, punk. You think this is funny, huh? Huh?" they barked, as I was being handcuffed, shackled in waist and leg irons, and finally hauled away.

I just kept on smiling. You see, they had no idea what I had just been through at Rikers. At that point in time, nothing could shake me. Nothing could break me. There was absolutely nothing they could do to get a rise out of me. Well, except for this one thing....

"Aww, Your First Orange Jumpsuit"

Yep, it was time to give up those street clothes. With the exception of the gray "I'm a psycho" jumpsuit I had to wear while being transported out of suicide watch, we were allowed to wear our street clothes at Rikers. Not so at county jail.

I was taken to an intake area by one of the county COs and allowed to take a shower, which I was pretty excited about until I jumped in and realized there was nothing but ice-cold water. When I got out of the shower, I was given an orange jumpsuit and a pair of sandals, or "bobos," as detainees called them, in exchange for all of my street clothes. That meant I was wearing just the orange jumpsuit with no underwear or socks. About twenty-four hours later, I was hauled off to the courtroom by none other than Sergeant "Wyatt Earp" for my arraignment hearing. What's an arraignment hearing, you ask?

A felony arraignment is one of the first steps in the process of being formally charged with a felony. The main purpose of the arraignment hearing is to apprise defendants of their constitutional rights under the Sixth Amendment, which is the right to be informed of the crime they are being accused of. During this hearing, a defendant typically comes into contact with the attorney who will be prosecuting the case against him for the first time.

So there I was, standing in a courtroom full of people, wearing no underwear or socks, in a jumpsuit that was two sizes too big for me. I could feel the breeze blowing through the snap-on buttons of my jumpsuit, around my genitals, and over my naked ass. I couldn't fucking believe it. My attorney, whom I hadn't seen since my homecoming, kept trying to whisper to me about my case, but I was having a hard time concentrating on anything but the awkwardness of the situation.

I thought the absence of dignity I experienced at Rikers Island had been the pinnacle of condescension, but this balls-swinging-in-the-breeze arraignment hearing was pretty darned offensive and ranked high on the humiliation scale. Assuming it was indeed deliberate, it was a great lesson in humiliation. Chalk up a few points for Wyatt Earp and the county intimidation squad. Well played, boys.

The County Holding Tank

I was taken to a holding tank until the "Keystone Cops" could decide what to do with me. Wow, this was real chicken shit compared to my New York journey. Guys doing weekends for unpaid child support, drunk and disorderly overnighters, guys picked up on petty warrants—just a bunch of crapola offenses and general bullshit. But to me it was paradise, as far as incarceration goes. There was "nothing to fear but fear itself." I used the time to catch up on some well-needed rest and relaxation. The food was a notch better than the Rikers slop, too. You've got to love them gel-laden spam sandwiches and those soggy frozen fish sticks. Yum.

I must have come close to breaking the record for the longest stay in the county holding tank at about ten days. I think this was also supposed to intimidate me. Sorry guys, no dice. The bare-balls courtroom experience might have gotten me, but I was as happy as a clam in that tank.

You see, I received the brunt of an increased animosity level because I had been a public official. Some of the county officials loved to hate me, some of them just wanted to put on a good show for the public, and some were just caught up in the moment. You know what I mean. Everyone loves to hate a bad politician, government official, IRS agent, or motor vehicles worker, and it was my turn to be besmirched and lambasted.

The Freddy Coreman Rule Book

I was finally released from the holding cell and taken up to my tier. It was the designated high-crime unit that housed the most serious criminal element in the county—the *real* bad guys—theoretically. Compared to where I had just come from, the county jail bar was set pretty low. I quickly learned that the majority of the guys on this tier were paper tigers and guys whose bark was bigger than their bite, with a few notable exceptions. Rumor had it that the worst of the detainees was Freddy Coreman. I'm sure it was no accident that they assigned me to his cell.

Freddy was a middle-aged man who had been in and out of prison most of his life for various charges of assault, concealed weapons, and robbery, and the felonious list goes on. He was also an ex-marine and a serious Bible thumper. He would be my cellmate for my first few months at the county facility.

This guy was one of a kind. The combination of being black and oppressed, an ex-marine, and an expert on prison etiquette made for a glaringly unique individual. There was only one way to do things in Freddy's cell—his way. He had the most myopic, lopsided perspective of the world of anyone I had ever met. I don't know whether it was the US Marine Corps, his years of incarceration, or what, but it was like a proper-procedure manual had been embedded into his brain, and there was absolutely no room left for anything else. As an example of everyday life with Freddy, here are some of his basic rules:

1. Bare feet and bare socks are never allowed to touch concrete—floors or walls or ceilings.
2. Asses, clothed or not, are never allowed to touch *anything* except your own bed and a toilet seat—and even then, there are specific rules that must be followed. What about chairs, you ask? Yes, but only after placing a towel down first. (By the way, this is why he would stand up at meal times. Too many asses on benches and no towels allowed in the lunch area.)
3. Hands can touch only your bed, toilet paper, and your own food. You can also touch the toilet handle or knobs of a faucet, but they must be meticulously cleaned afterward. No handshaking, item sharing, or touching. Not even an accidental brushing. I later learned that the proper medical term for this is "mysophobia," more commonly known as "germophobia."

4. Towels, used or not, cannot touch anything but you or your bed. If you have a spare, you can use it exclusively for sitting on.

OK, now let's apply these rules to something as simple as getting up out of bed and getting dressed each morning. I had the top bunk (no ladders, by the way; it's jail, not television). Try to envision the planning involved in simply getting down from the top bunk and over to the toilet, which I had to do at least a few times a night and in the morning:

- I had to sleep with my clothes, towel, sandals, and socks up on my bunk so I could put them on before making my way down to the floor. On the top bunk, there's only about two or three feet between you and the ceiling, so I had to put on my orange jumpsuit, socks, and shoes while crouched or lying down.
- Now, I couldn't dangle my legs over the edge of the bed. That would put my feet in Freddy's space, and they might actually touch his portion of the bedframe. That meant I had to fling myself off the top bunk sideways and twist around in midair to land upright and on my feet—with my towel in hand, of course.
- Then I could step over to the toilet to pee. First, I had to wipe down the seat with paper towels, then pee, then wipe it all down again. The same thing at the sink: wipe the knobs down, turn them on, wash up, then turn them off and clean them again with paper towels.

All the while, Freddy was watching my every move to make sure I didn't miss a beat. Unlike me, who preferred to sleep as late as I possibly could in the morning, Freddy was up every morning before 6:00 a.m. like clockwork, so there was no getting around it. This morning ritual was just the tip of the iceberg of peculiar rules, oddball philosophies, and plain old crazy shit this guy lived by. Like the double standard, good Christian versus hard-ass criminal mind-set he had. He was oblivious to it, but one minute he was quoting from the New Testament with fortitude and righteousness, and the next minute he was telling you to fuck off and that he was going to kick the piss out of you.

I firmly believe the powers that be wanted to make things as difficult as possible for me by assigning me to Freddy's cell, and they might have succeeded. However, even with all the bullshit I had to put up with as Freddy's bunkie, I still felt as if the county facility was summer camp compared to Rikers Island. With Rikers as a benchmark, it's tough to feel much in the way of grief.

After a few weeks, I actually began to take Freddy in stride and became more of an ally and a kind-of-sort-of friend to him. He wasn't used to a guy like me. First, I knew about and could talk to him about Christianity. Second, I knew the criminal justice system and could help him with his legal issues. Third, I was willing to share my commissary with him. You see, to buy from the commissary, someone from the outside has to deposit money into your jail account and Freddy had no one willing or able to do so. Did his quirks and phobias make me crazy at times? Absolutely. But things gradually settled into a relatively peaceful coexistence between us—probably even better than most of the other cellmates on the tier. Other detainees who had been on the tier for a long while were amazed that I lasted as long as I did in Freddy's cell, which was about two months total. Apparently, prior to me, the longest anyone had lasted was a few weeks.

I eventually left Freddy's cell and was assigned to another one. This time, I was with a skinhead guy in his thirties named Julian. Talk about one extreme to the other.

Who's Got Your Back?

Dinner was over, and I headed to the second floor of the tier to my favorite spot, the balcony outside of the bathroom adjacent to my cell. A group of us would hang out in that area—mostly the older detainees like me and a few of the younger, white-collar-crime guys. For obvious reasons, we had some things in common. Naturally, you flock toward those whom you can actually have a seminormal conversation with. What a great vantage point the balcony was. We could see the entire tier down below and catch all the action from "on high."

This new guy showed up right before dinner. He was a white guy in his thirties who was about six feet two and built like a brick shithouse. No one knew his name. He had a real fucked-up attitude. As he was going into the bathroom next to where we were all sitting, he looked at all five of us sitting there and said, "Hey, you assholes better be gone when I get out of the shower."

Our space on the balcony had been established long before he arrived, and running off like a bunch of wimps would not have earned us any points with the guys on the tier. We all ignored him and assumed he was full of shit.

But when he came out of the bathroom, he made a mad dash toward us and immediately threw two guys to the floor. They both scampered away, one of them with a serious bloody nose and mouth. The three of us who were left stood our ground for about thirty seconds, until he had two more guys down. Even with the three of us all over him, this guy managed to bash the heads of my last two accomplices into the second-floor metal guard railing, and they were pretty much down for the count.

That left me. Me versus this fucking freight train on steroids. As he lunged toward me, I knew I was about to receive one hell of a beating. But then, all of a sudden, he stopped about three feet in front of me and just froze. I quickly realized he was looking at something behind me, and I heard a voice say, "You touch him, and I'll break your fucking neck, Evans."

Evans? Who the fuck is Evans? I thought. Mr. Brick-Shithouse responded with, "Holy shit. If it ain't Freddy fucking Coreman?"

Yep, it was Freddy. He grabbed me by the collar of my jumpsuit and firmly shoved me aside. Then, staring at each other nose to nose, Freddy said to Evans, "I almost killed you last time. This time will be for real."

Evans just smirked and walked away. He never came near me or anyone else on the tier again. It turns out that Freddy and Evans knew each other from a previous stint in state prison, where Freddy ended up doing some extra time behind bars for the same kind of thing; protecting his cellmate and beating Evans half to death.

Freddy surprised the hell out of me that day, and he taught me something about alliances in jail. At the time of this confrontation, we weren't cellmates anymore, and I spoke to him only on occasion. There were actually three lessons to be learned here:

1. In jail, you quickly find out who your friends are.
2. Be thankful you have them.

3. Don't second-guess anyone who's bigger, younger, and meaner than you are because, in jail, nobody's gonna back down.

Tattoos and Broken Hearts

I was moved to a new cell with my new cellmate, Julian. He was considered to be someone you didn't want to mess with, mostly because of his supposed skinhead status and his several swastika tattoos. In actuality, he was a quiet guy who mostly kept to himself, and if you left him alone, he would leave you alone. In time, I learned that the only thing that I had to worry about was his temper, which could be highly volatile and dangerous. Julian was an excellent artist—and I mean excellent! He put this talent to good use in county jail as the resident tattoo guy. It was illegal as hell to give or receive tattoos in the county jail, but guys managed to find ways of doing it anyway. I'm sure that's no big surprise to anyone. To make his tattoo ink, Julian would covertly stick a paper clip into an electrical outlet to create a spark to burn a wad of paper. He would then immediately whisk the burning paper into our cell and into the metal sink, using his body to mask the burning paper from the guard's desk. After multiple attempts, he would collect enough soot from the burning paper to mix it with baby oil, although in desperation, I saw him use the oil from a tuna packet a few times. I even saw him add beet juice and soap to the equation to obtain a nice, deep, purple-colored ink for special occasions, like the broken heart he would eventually put on his own forearm.

Julian wouldn't talk to me for the first few weeks I was in his cell. We just stayed out of each other's way. Slowly but surely, we began to break the ice. What started the icebreaker was a letter he received. I watched him stare at this letter for days, and I wondered what the hell had him so mesmerized. About three days into this letter obsession, we were lying in our bunks after the 10:00 p.m. lights-out announcement when he said his first words to me: "Can you read?" he asked.

"What?" I said, not sure I heard him right.

Then he said, "Will you read this letter for me and tell me exactly what it means?"

I was a bit perplexed and cautious as he handed the letter down to me from the top bunk. As I began to read it, I realized that this was not going to go over well with Julian. I started wondering how I was going to break it to him without him flipping out or killing me in my sleep. It was a letter from the courts about the custody of the three-year-old child he apparently had on the outside.

Basically, it said that his spouse had filed a motion to have him, the incarcerated father, stripped of his custody and decision-making rights for his child. It went on to say that a correspondence and telephone restriction was being placed on Julian so there would be no communicating with the mother or the child. *Oh God, here goes*, I thought as I began to tell him the bad news.

He didn't do anything or say a word in response—not even a question or clarification—nothing. That night, I heard him crying above me in his bunk, and he just kept repeating his baby's name: "Frankie, he's *my* little Frankie." Wow, I felt terrible for him. He was absolutely devastated.

The next morning at breakfast, with all of his pent-up anger and frustration, Julian picked a guy up off his seat and slammed him against the wall just for asking him about a tattoo. No COs were around, so there were no consequences. He stayed in the cell for the next few days, missing most meals and recreation time. I had an idea. I wanted to help him, but I was a little afraid to broach the subject of the letter.

Finally, a few days later, after lights out, I mustered up the strength to blurt out, "Julian, you need to respond to that fucking letter. You need to tell the courts that you refuse to relinquish your child-custody rights and that you're willing to fight for them. You need to tell them that you will be out of here in a year, and you intend to see your child and that nothing will stop you."

Realizing what I was saying, I then said, "And I will write the letter for you. OK?"

There was silence at first, and I didn't know what to expect from him, so I cringed as he jumped down from his bunk. He crouched down and stared straight at me. Well, I'll be damned. I think it was the first time I had ever seen this man smile. He just looked at me straight in the face and said, "You are a good person" and proceeded to sit on the floor in the darkness, once again staring at the infamous letter.

I swear to God, in the morning he was still sitting there, staring at me and waiting for me to get up. Like a five-year-old waiting for Christmas morning. No breakfast that day. We stayed in the cell and wrote our first letter to the courts. That morning, I learned that Frankie lived out of state with his mom, about five hundred miles away. Julian had a notebook with an X on each page that he'd been in jail so he could keep track of how many days he had been away from Frankie. That's right. Nothing but one big X on the front and back of each page. I was afraid to ask what he was going to do when he ran out of pages.

Fast-forward three months, two appearances, and two letters later—I was no longer in Julian's cell. It was the day he left the county facility for state prison that he received a notice from the courts that he would retain most of his custody rights. He practically ran over to my cell with the letter. I read it to him and told him the good news. He showed me the new tattoo he had put on his left arm. It was a broken heart with an arrow going through it, of course. A few hours later, he was off to state prison.

Being a realist, I prayed that he might actually get to see Frankie again someday. Some guys celebrate life by getting a tattoo. As for me, I write a song.

Tattoos and Broken Hearts

Tattoos and broken hearts and shattered dreams and we're worlds apart,
Hey, I can't remember if I told you, I've been longing just to hold you.
My child, my heart, my life, I don't want to live another day without...
Hey, I put your name on my new tattoo,
It's a broken heart with an arrow going through.

Tattoos and broken hearts, I'm counting every day that we're apart,
five hundred miles away from you,
Tattoos and broken hearts, I dream about the new life we will start;
'til then there's nothing I can do...so I got a new tattoo...and I did it just for you.

Cheese Wars

I had a cellmate, or bunkie as the young guys referred to them, who was like a character plucked out of some 1980s TV sitcom. He was a spirited black guy in his early forties named Willy. He was a plain old unintimidating and strangely funny guy. He seemed to be taking the whole prison experience in stride with a positive attitude I found uplifting in the midst of the chaos and heartache that permeates the air of incarceration. Then again, there were times when his glaringly ethnic phraseology and deep Southern accent were almost impossible for me to understand.

Willy and I always seemed to talk about the same three things: good sex, good food, and the pleasure of a nice, stiff drink. We both agreed that these were the three things we missed the most on the outside. Yes, he was a man after my own heart. He would ask me to tell him about my Italian heritage and how to prepare classics like pizza and pasta. Sometimes I'd tell him about good Italian wines and cheeses, too. One day, he told me that his favorite Italian cheese was "Farmer John" cheese. Not to insult him, I just went along with him and said, "Oh yeah, that's great."

For more than a week, he kept rambling on and on about this supposedly Italian Farmer John cheese. It was driving me crazy. Finally, one day I told him I really didn't know what the hell he was talking about and that there was no such thing as Farmer John cheese in Italy or anywhere else, for that matter. Man, did he get pissed. My "funny, high-spirited" Willy erupted like a volcano. It was tough enough to understand him when he wasn't rambling on like a lunatic, but this was even worse.

Eventually, I was able to make out his words. It was when he said, "What kind of Italian are you? Italians sprinkle Farmer John cheese over macaroni and pizza and garlic bread and everything. They put that damned Farmer John cheese on everything."

Bingo! There it was. He was talking about Italian parmigiana cheese! "Farmer John" was "parmi-gian." Damn, how could I have missed that?

As we stood and argued in the rec area, our vigorous "battle of the cheeses" attracted lots of attention from the guys on the tier, and some were shouting out the typical "kick his ass" and "fuck him up" bullshit. Instead, I apologized to Willy, and we shook hands and walked back into our cell. Willy and I were buddies again and peace descended upon cell number twenty-four.

A few minutes later, Willy looked over at me with a big, goofy smile on his face and said, "So what's your favorite position?"

Survival and Finding Your Niche

Like anything else in this world, everything naturally settles into its place. In the realm of physics, they say, "One change is continually balanced by another to form a steady state." In society, we all eventually find our "steady state." For the purposes of this section, let's just call it a niche. It's the place where we feel safe and are most comfortable. As a matter of survival, we gravitate toward what we are familiar with and seek shelter from the storm of unfamiliarity and uncertainty swirling around us. That's what is going on in prison—and for good reason.

As a matter of survival, you must find your niche and identify where you fit on the food chain. Top, middle, or bottom of the chain doesn't matter so much as establishing an identity that affords you the latitude you need to survive. The best way to develop this latitude is to have something to offer. Inmates want to know what *you* can do for *them*, like whether you've got something they may need in the future, or why they shouldn't mess with you, and what they stand to lose if they do. If you think you'll just hang around and be a nice guy like you did on the outside and everything will be OK, you're wrong. Find your niche, and fast. Then you've got to live *with* it and live *by* it. In incarceration, everything is considered a serious matter, and your word must always be as good as gold.

Bang, Bang Maxwell's Silver Hammer—I Mean, Ice Pick

Max was a young guy I met in the county jail facility. All of us so-called high-profile-crime guys were housed together in the same block and were considered to be the real bad guys. Max had been incarcerated since the age of fifteen. He was transferred from a youth correctional facility to the county jail while awaiting his trial for the violent assault of his forty-something-year-old neighbor. We'll call her Mary. The story, as it was conveyed to me, goes something like this.

Fifteen-year-old Max had robbed Mary's house earlier in the week of the assault and was feeling way too paranoid for his own good. Instead of steering clear of Mary and her house and trying to remain incognito like most common-sensible people would, he had a better idea. He decided he was going to watch Mary's every move. After all, if he didn't keep an eye on her, she might just figure out what he did. Well, you get the picture.

Paranoia's a bitch. One day after a few hits of his big brother's crystal meth and a few too many beers, he went outside to "man his post" behind the fence and keep an eye on Mary, 'cause you just never know. As she pulled into her driveway, she made the big, big mistake of noticing Max behind the fence and simply saying, "Hey, I know it's you, Max. Come out, Max, I know it's you. Come on, I know it's you." Max flipped out. She said she knew it was him! Oh, no, he was sure Mary must know what he did!

As the story goes, when the ambulance arrived, they found Mary at her doorstep bathed in blood, clutching onto her house keys and her life. Later, the official count was somewhere around thirty stab wounds, mostly to the face. Although she would survive the assault, plastic surgery could hardly repair the devastating damage done to Mary's face.

Max was found and arrested days later with a homemade silver-handled ice pick in his back pocket. When the police questioned him, his only reason for attacking Mary was, supposedly, "I didn't want her to tell Mom that I robbed her house."

Max found his niche in county jail with the small but fear-provoking "skinhead" group of guys, and he settled in with his "protector," Big John. Max was like Big John's "Mini Me." I was transferred to their cell before I left county jail—it was Big John, Little Max, and me.

About three weeks later, Max and I happened to get shipped off to state prison on the same day. We arrived and were placed in the same cell at the state assignment facility. For three days, as we awaited placement into our final resting place (meaning which state prison facility we'd be assigned to), Max spent his days in a mental frenzy, staring out through the bars and struggling like a caged monkey, trying to figure out who and what he could latch on to. Mini Me was all alone now and couldn't bear the feeling of just being plain old Max—no protector, no skinheads, no silver ice pick to protect him.

On our last day in that cell, as we were being moved and separated, I looked back at Max and said, "Stay cool, Max. I believe you're about to learn something. The world is a cold place when it's just me, myself, and I," to which he had no reply. But I'll never forget the puzzled look on his face.

Sanity 101: Life in a Concrete Box

You've got to deal with it. Each day you fight another battle within yourself. This battle consists of everything from confrontation to condemnation to deprivation. First, you're constantly confronted by detainees who are naturally compelled to test and challenge you. Second, some of the COs consider it their purpose in life to rub your nose in the helplessness and condemnation you've earned in your new life of incarceration. Last but not least, you're deprived of your freedom of choice in just about everything you do, when you do it, how you do it, and whom you do it with.

Do you know how many times I've had people ask, "So, how do you handle it day after day after day?" The mere thought of life in a six-by-ten concrete box scares the hell out of anyone who hasn't been there. That is indeed understandable, and before I had actually experienced it firsthand, I couldn't even fathom the *idea* of incarceration, let alone imagine myself actually living the miserable day-to-day life of a prison inmate. However, the mind is a powerful instrument. Almost immediately, I learned that I had this amazing, built-in defense mechanism that I was completely unaware of prior to my incarceration. This unanticipated defense mode kicked in as soon as my jailbird journey began back in Rikers Island.

The bottom line is that most of us are a lot stronger inside than we realize. What I mean is that if you're forced into a situation, or a place, or a life-changing event, it's amazing how you find the strength and resilience to move beyond the fray. Prison is most definitely one of those life-changing events, and just like anything else in this world, most of us find a way to manage our emotions and fears in an admirable way when circumstances, as horrifying as they may be, jump out and smack us in the face. To put it another way, it's a metamorphosis, like a soldier who steps onto the battlefield for the first time. His senses and his defenses are heightened, and he is transformed from Joe Freedom to Joe Survival.

Of course there are exceptions to every rule...

Crazy Billy

Like me, Billy was one of the only four guys at the county facility who was over forty-five years old during our fabulous stay. We got to be fairly good buddies and celled together for a few months. It's a godsend when you end up with a cellmate you get along with and actually have some things in common with. The only problem with Billy was that he just couldn't get over the fact that he was there.

Night and day, in or out of the cell, he walked around talking about how he was wronged, how he didn't do it, and how he was going to kill himself if he had to stay one minute longer in jail. He used to say, "Today is the day I'm going to jump head-first from the second-floor tier." It was mostly bullshit, but I always felt there was a tinge of reality in there somewhere.

Some of the guys got so tired of hearing him that they would egg him on, chanting things like, "Go, Billy, go! It's time to start the show!" I warned him, as did many others, that he'd better not let the guards hear him say anything about killing himself, or he would be facing some time in the isolation unit, more commonly known at the county facility as solitary confinement. But Billy wouldn't listen.

One day, while sitting and eating dinner, three guards grabbed Billy and hauled him off to the isolation unit. He was gone for about twelve days. After being OK'd by somebody, probably some psych nurse, he came back to the tier. He wouldn't talk to anyone; not even the old "I'm going to kill myself" words came out of his mouth.

I tried to talk to him a few times and figure out what the hell had happened to him in isolation, but I got nowhere. He was just "different." He walked around with this crazed, half-smile kind of look on his face and stayed pretty much to himself. The guy I had known a few weeks earlier was gone. I started getting really creeped out by him. It was strange as hell.

That was when I had one of the worst fucking nightmares I've ever had in my life. In the dream, Billy leaped off the second-floor tier. He grabbed onto a hanging light fixture. As the sparking electrical wires began to weaken and stretch, it became obvious that he was soon going to fall.

He swung back and forth for a minute, screaming at the top of his lungs, "Fuck you, fuck me, fuck you, fuck me!"

In my dream, Billy hit the floor flat on his back and just laid there convulsing. I ran down to the first floor and reached down to try to help him. When I grabbed his hand, I began to be electrocuted and burned as Billy opened his eyes and laughed hysterically back at me. This "convulsive electrocution state" went on for what seemed like forever. When I finally woke up, my body was still shaking, and I felt as if I'd just been put through a meat grinder.

Here's the clincher. When I sat up from my bunk and looked up, Billy was peering in at me through the portal in the cell door, just watching me with that fucked-up psycho look on his face. I'm no horror-film fanatic, but it was like something out of *The Shining*, with Billy taking the role of Jack Nicholson.

Who's Judge Mental?

No one is off-limits. "Judge Mental" was the name earned by one of the judges who presided over all of us so-called scumbags awaiting trial at the county facility. I was told that he had earned his title for his harsh sentencing and apparent closed-minded attitude toward defendants in his courtroom. Statistically, his sentencing was alleged to be more severe than most judges in other counties in the state. In simple terms, the detainees considered him to be a notorious hard-ass.

Throughout this book, I've been preaching about certain injustices and flaws that stem from our not-so-perfect sentencing process. Judge Mental's tale is a shining example of that flaw. As I've said before, my only issue is that the punishment should fit the crime —not maybe, or sometimes, or it depends, but always. As one detainee so eloquently put it, Judge Mental was "doling out sentences that didn't fit anything but local politics and the length of his middle finger."

Like what, you ask? Well, things like giving a guy on his last month of probation five years for possession of an ounce of pot, a half gram of cocaine, and being under the same roof as his brother, who owned a hunting rifle locked in the closet of another room. Things like finding some convoluted way to give a guy six years for possession of a stolen firearm that belonged to his roommate—with paperwork to prove it. It would appear that this decision had to do with the fact that the guy had been charged with possession in his past. Twelve years past.

Then there was the guy who got seven years for evading police and resisting arrest. This is a real classic. He was on his way home from his daughter's wedding, so he was wearing a tuxedo, and it was during a huge rainstorm. The officers followed him for a while on suspicion he'd been drinking, pulled him over, and ordered him to get out of the car. He did, but when the officers ordered him to lie on the ground, which would have been smack dab in the middle of a mud puddle, he refused. There was a scuffle as two officers wrestled him to the ground. The officers later claimed that this guy didn't pull over soon enough after the red lights went on, and he ended up with some trumped-up charges of evading police and resisting arrest.

I could go on and on. I could also tell you more about the other end of the spectrum—those who deserved to be there for a long time, such as the child molesters, rapists, and other violent-crime guys who received lesser sentences—but I won't.

Suffice it to say that I cringed when I saw those low-life bastards fly through the system, given the shit they had done. One-year county stints and three-year state bids were doled out to some of these guys as if they had done nothing but stolen a candy bar. Others like me and some of the guys I've mentioned became the sad recipients of that "Judge Mental"-style, middle-finger justice system. Sure, we did it. We committed the crime, but not five, six, and seven years' worth. No way.

Go, Johnny, Go

Johnny was a great guy, someone who stood out from the rest of the guys on the tier, like me, mainly because he was a little older than most of the others. But it was more than just that. He was smart, and his life experiences provided him with a diversity of knowledge on many levels. He knew about everything from computers to jigsaws to crack cocaine, and I learned a few things from him about all three.

Johnny's the guy who was on his way home from his daughter's wedding in his tuxedo during a huge rainstorm and got seven years for evading police and resisting arrest.

Now, here's the inside scoop. In truth, Johnny actually did push the limits and consciously avoided pulling over for the cops that night. He eventually did pull over, but when the cop flicked on the red lights and started after him, he traveled a few miles until he got to his house before doing so. Why would Johnny do that?

Well, sometimes things are just too simple to mince words. Now, brace yourself. He got deathly ill from something he ate at the wedding and was on the verge of shitting his pants. He needed to get to a toilet ASAP, plain and simple. When he arrived at his house, he didn't stand around to chat with the pursuing officer. He made a mad dash inside the house and to the toilet to relieve himself. When he returned outside minutes later, four squad cars were waiting for him instead of one. You know the rest of the story. It doesn't end well.

So, should Johnny have stopped for the officer and just shit his pants in the car? I'm not so sure if I would have. Well, actually, I don't think so. It's easy to second-guess these things, but I know the last thing Johnny expected was that the events of that infamous night would escalate into a bunch of "resisting arrest" charges and a prison sentence. Sometimes you just step in shit, no pun intended. Sometimes you're the victim of bad circumstances, and sometimes the collateral damage is unforeseeable.

Look, I know Johnny was no angel, but he wasn't a monster, either. I can only imagine what was going through his head as he was zipping down the road, gritting his teeth, trying to decide whether to stop or not, all the while trying his best not to shit his pants. It must have sucked to be Johnny that night, and in fact, I think Johnny deserved an award for being "number one father of the bride," although number two might be more appropriate. Go, Johnny, go.

The Flames of Desire

Some of the crazy shit that goes on at county jail is just too mind-blowing to be ignored. Certain detainees actually brought the word "innovation" to a whole new level. Here's an example that I call "the air-vent express."

There were a number of floors that housed detainees at the facility, each housing different factions of the criminal element, such as high crime, low crime, male, female, and non–US citizens. If you wanted to communicate with other detainees, there were basically three ways to do it:

1. You could hope to pass them when you were in transit throughout the facility—to and from court, visiting day, and recreation, for example.
2. You could hand a note to the guy from the kitchen who delivered the meals to each tier and offer him something to deliver your message for you.
3. You could use the air-vent express. This was done by using the HVAC vents that passed through each jail cell and each floor of the facility.

If you wanted to talk to a guy a couple of tiers away, you could pass your message to the guys in the cells directly above or below you, name the time and the two aligning cell numbers where you want to meet, and hold your "board meeting." Sometimes there would be multiple conversations going on at the same time. It was pretty eerie sounding with the effect that the airflow has on the audio. It reminded me of the sound we got when we used to speak into the room fan or air conditioner when I was a kid.

There were a variety of reasons to use this innovative communication option. As you might imagine, detainees did not normally end up on the same tier as their friends or codefendants, but they were determined to find a way to communicate with them to get their stories straight, and so on. The air-vent express was a perfect solution.

Then there were the guys who just wanted to talk to the women's tier. Didn't matter what woman; they just wanted to hear that female voice. It was about as close as they were going to get to normal sex. The women's tier must not have been aligned with the others because it was difficult to hear well, but when everyone was locked in their cells for the night, you could often hear some guy and some girl dirty talking their way through a mutual masturbation session. No one really talked about it much, but most every guy on the tier within earshot of these sessions had their heads pressed against their air vents for their own listening pleasure. As it turns out, so were the female detainees. Everyone needs to feed those flames of desire.

Lucky Charms

In jail, drugs were a significant part of everyday life. Even with all the precautions and procedures put in place by the department of corrections and county correctional facilities, there were guys who were able to "mouth" their prescribed drugs from the daily med line without being detected, as well as those who found other creative ways to get drugs into the facility. In some cases, like at Rikers Island, it's the COs who actually facilitated the smuggling, and they profit from it. In any case, drugs covertly appear and are bought, sold, and consumed, despite the best efforts of the powers that be.

That being said, there were serious consequences if you were caught with drugs in your possession, whether they were found on your body or in your cell. Although I often considered it, only on a few occasions did I actually participate in scoring and consuming these jailhouse drugs while I was incarcerated. During the first six months of my journey, there was a brief period of time when I jumped on the bandwagon, and I would get high as an escape. This was while I was still learning to deal with life as a jailbird and trying to cope with the realities of prison life. But that phase passed quickly as I began to realize how important it was to stay focused and strong. Being anesthetized and unfocused does nothing but make you vulnerable and weak. Those are the last two things you can afford to be during incarceration.

I had a cellmate who was trading his commissary items for drugs on a regular basis. He was getting enough Ativan tablets to last him a week at a time. I know they sometimes came from guys who mouthed them out of the med line, but there were too many of them floating around the tier for that to be his only source. They had to be coming in from other places as well.

One of the places I learned about was what some called the "chuck wagon." That's the guy who worked in the kitchen and brought the cart full of meal trays to our tier at meal times. Even though a CO accompanied the chuck wagon and stood there as the trays were doled out, the chuck wagon guy was able to hide drugs, mainly pills, in some very creative places in and around the food on the tray. He also managed to get the right tray to the right detainee, with some exceptions.

Sometimes things didn't go as planned. Like the time at breakfast when I received my box of cornflakes with about thirty tablets inside. Imagine my surprise when I poured my cornflakes into the bowl and noticed that they looked more like lucky charms with little pink and white marshmallow tablets floating on top. It's tough to know what to do when you're put on the spot like this. Trying to avoid the potential "guilt by association," the guys on either side of me got a glimpse of my lucky charms, stood up, and promptly moved the fuck away from me.

Before I got to the panic point, the intended recipient of the lucky charms swooped behind me, grabbed the food tray, tossed down another one, and kept moving as inconspicuously as he could to another table. The expectation is that no one will open their mouth about these kinds of incidents. Those who do will be considered a snitch, and let's just say they will pay a heavy price.

For obvious reasons, at the county jail, you're waiting for your sentencing hearing, trying to figure out what your sentence will be and where you'll be sent. You and your fellow detainees are constantly talking about the different state prisons you might end up in, which are the best, which are the worst, and which ones house inmates of your particular variety.

Well, the length of your sentence, the prison you are assigned to, and your eligibility for parole are all influenced to some extent by your behavior while in county jail. So if you're constantly getting into trouble, whether it's fighting, drugs, or any other infraction, you're essentially putting at risk your chances of keeping your prison sentence to a minimum.

Although I would encourage anyone new to incarceration to do whatever they need to do to command respect, it doesn't mean you have to be stupid. Staying focused and strong and fighting to protect yourself are essential (to whatever extent it may be necessary). But if getting the hell out of there is your priority, or clearing the way for the best possible ride as you move through the court system, messing with drugs is going to get you nowhere. Hey, I had lots of intoxicating cravings and fixations. Man, I couldn't wait to get home and regain my freedom to indulge in a few stiff drinks. But that's the key. Focus on getting home first and having fun later.

Sticky Fingers

One fine afternoon, about an hour after lunch, my cellmate showed me the new stash of pills he had just scored. OK, this was his normal routine, and I didn't really give a damn. I just sat there reading the magazine I was reading without giving it much thought. Sure, if you get caught with medication or contraband in your cell, you're toast, but I took the attitude that it was his problem, not mine. He took his stash of pills and casually stuck them under his pillow on the bottom bunk and said, "Hey, I'll hide these pills when I get back. I'm going to go take a shower before lockdown," and he walked out the door. No big deal, right?

Wrong! A few minutes after he walked out the door, all hell broke loose. The COs launched into a surprise inspection, ordering everyone to exit and stand against the wall outside their cell. As I leaped off my top bunk, I could hear the yelling and the slamming doors down the hall as the COs began to storm into everyone's cell for inspection. With only seconds to burn before they would arrive at my cell, I stood there panicking about what the fuck I should do about the drugs they would easily find sitting there under the pillow of the bottom bunk. You see, it didn't matter where in the cell drugs were found; both cellmates would be sent to "the hole" and charged with an infraction.

I was lucky that my cell was at the end of the hall because it gave me a few extra seconds to grab the stash of pills, stuff them in my sock, and sprint out of the cell and stand against the wall, as ordered. Then we were all asked to sit down on the floor and wait until the cell inspections were finished, at which time they would body-search us for contraband.

Another stroke of luck was that my cell was located on a portion of the tier where there happened to be a small section of carpeting. As I sat there waiting for the cell inspection to be over and our "grab your knees" inspection to begin, I inconspicuously struggled to tear the carpeting I was sitting on from the edge of the floor. My plan was to move the pills from my sock and shove them under the carpet so they wouldn't find them during the upcoming body search. My heart pounded as I finally managed to get the plastic baggy full of pills under the carpet and the carpet pressed back firmly on top of them.

Then I felt something wet on my fingers and noticed that the fingers of my right hand were bleeding. The tack strip that holds the carpeting down had badly sliced up the tips of my fingers while I was struggling to rip up the edge of the carpet. By the time I even realized what happened to my fingers, the COs were upon us.

They ordered, "Stand up and put your hands against the wall!" We did. Then they ordered us to "turn around and put your hands behind your back!" We did. "What the fuck?" one of the cops shouted at me as he looked up and saw partial handprints of blood on the wall. He looked at my hands and asked me why the fuck I was bleeding.

I hesitated for a few seconds and said, "I slammed my fingers in the cell door."

"What?" he asked in disbelief. "How the hell do you bleed from slamming the cell door on your fingers?"

I hesitated again and said, "I don't know." I felt like a guilty five-year-old lying about who stole the cookies from the cookie jar. I prayed he wouldn't think to glance downward and notice that the edge of the carpet looked a little ruffled.

He put his face a few inches from mine and said, "You're full of shit," as the sergeants started calling the COs up to the next floor. He slowly walked away, occasionally looking back at me and making one of those two-fingers-to-his-eyes pointing gestures, indicating that he would be watching me. Damn!

It was over, and we were ordered back into our cells. Besides washing the blood off my fingers, there was only one thing on my mind as I lay there in my bunk staring at the ceiling. I wanted to "kill" my bunkie for putting me through this whole drug-stashing, finger-bleeding nightmare.

As my bunkie walked into the room, fresh from the shower with a big smile on his face, he asked, "I heard all kinds of commotion out here while I was in the shower. What the hell happened?"

I wanted so badly to just punch him in the stomach, but I didn't. Instead, I just looked him in the eye, wiped the remaining blood on my fingers across the towel he was wearing, and answered, "Inspection."

"Holy shit, that's blood. Are you fucking crazy?" he asked. Then it hit him. His eyes flung open like he'd seen a ghost, and he lunged over to look under his pillow for the stash of pills.

"Damn it! Those sons of bitches must have taken them!" he yelled.

"Yeah, they must have," I said, acting as if I gave a shit.

He looked puzzled and whispered, "I wonder why they didn't bust us. I'll bet they kept them for themselves!"

"Yeah, you can't trust those slimy CO bastards," I whispered back. Yeah, right. Dream on, pal. That's just what the COs need—a handful of your tainted and stained Ativan tablets.

The next day, I made an excellent deal with the druggie two cells down. He got a cute little hand-drawn buried-treasure map, and I got enough Ramen noodles, corn chips, peanut butter, and coffee to last two weeks.

Derik Wedbetter

This guy was a classic. He'd lived 90 percent of his life in prison, from childhood through adulthood, and it showed. Wheeling and dealing was his thing, 24/7, and he knew nothing else. Everything was on the table, meaning that he'd trade merchandise, medication, favors, advice—anything. He had developed this keen ability to assess his fellow detainees and scope out their assets, formulate a deal and plan of attack, and then zero in on them for the kill.

Now, everyone bartered with commissary items such as coffee, cereal, and cookies, or toiletries like deodorant, shampoo, and foot powder, but Derik went way beyond that. He had an obsession. He was truly on the fringe.

Here's an example. I once witnessed a deal he made with another detainee that went something like this: "You give me two cinnamon rolls, two cereals, five postage stamps, and three envelopes from commissary, and I'll give you a lorazepam (the daily meds he mouthed and saved for bartering) and today's lunch tray, and I'll wash your socks and underwear for a week." When the guy said no, Derik said, "OK, my bunkie owes me a package of coffee. You can have that, too." That sealed the deal.

The first time he ever said a word to me, he had already determined my greatest jail "asset," which was my education and legal knowledge. Yes, my niche at that point was my ability to help detainees with legal work, letter writing, and even education, like getting their GED. He offered me two Twix bars, his dinner tray for the next two nights, and two lorazepam tablets if I would help him with his case and prepare two letters to the public defender for him.

Thinking he was a blatant lunatic, I initially told him to take a hike. He was relentless and became a real pain in the ass. He was up to four more candy bars, dinners, and lorazepam tablets when I finally decided to talk to him and see why he was so desperate.

What I discovered was that he was smart as hell about the law—the court system, in particular. He knew the judicial process, his legal rights, and exactly what he wanted to convey to his public defender. He had some clever ideas and arguments to help his case. I finally asked why the hell he didn't just write his own letters and leave me out of it. He just kept talking and ignored my question. I kept asking, and he kept ignoring.

Finally, he lost it. He started banging his fists on the table we were sitting at and screamed, "Because I can't...because I fucking can't! Are you happy now? I fucking can't!" Then he just sat there quietly, holding his head, huffing and puffing and staring down at the floor. Everyone within earshot of us turned around and stared.

Wow, I felt like a real asshole. It just never occurred to me that this poor guy couldn't write. He was smart as a whip about the law, but being behind bars practically all of his life, he never learned to read or write at more than about a third-grade level. His extensive legal knowledge of the law was beyond mine in many ways, and it came entirely from all of his years of incarceration—no books, no classrooms, no teachers. Just plain old firsthand experience, hearsay, and observation of the criminal justice system in action.

Here's the point. Some guys behind bars are pretty damned smart, but some of them just don't have the education to better themselves. During incarceration, this problem may keep them from getting out of prison because they don't have the tools to work their way toward release. On the outside, this problem may keep them from being able to stay out of prison because they don't have the tools to survive in a highly competitive society. It's just another dose of hard, cold reality and the adulterated virtues of humanity.

The next day, I wrote Derik's letters for him. And, no, I didn't ask for any candy bars, dinners, or lorazepam tablets in return.

Johnny Cakes

Johnny was a twenty-five-year-old from the most rural of rural areas in the state. He used to take that crappy assed Wonder Bread from his lunch and dinner trays, smash it up into doughy putty, and then flatten it into the shape of pancakes. Hence the nickname Johnny Cakes. On top of them, he would then squeeze honey, ketchup, mustard, and peanut butter packets from his commissary, and that's about all he ever seemed to eat. He traded most of his lunch and dinner trays for more Wonder Bread and condiment packets.

I'm sorry, but this guy brought new meaning to the term "dumber than dumb." We were all sitting around the one television we had on the tier, and Jerry Springer was on. Of course, there was a big messy, f-you confrontation on screen about who the father was of this whacko woman's baby. She was yelling and screaming and running around the stage, swinging at everyone in sight. You guessed it; it was time to read the DNA results of the three "who-be-duh-daddy" candidates who were all crouching down in their chairs in complete denial.

The guys on the tier loved to watch this shit, and so did little Johnny Cakes. He was getting real riled up and clenching his fists at the TV, and then he said it. The dumbest thing I'd ever heard came out of his mouth: "Them bitches, them bitches is all the same, why don't they never make them bitches take a DNA test? Why is it always the dude, huh, huh? Them bitches ain't no saints. Why don't they never make them take a paternity test?"

Everyone fell silent for half a minute with looks of disbelief on their faces, trying to digest what they had just heard. The show was over, and as everyone was getting up and walking away, someone said, "Johnny Cakes, you're about ten pancakes short of a stack," and everyone busted out laughing. Confused, Johnny Cakes turned back at everyone, asking, "What? Whaddaya mean? Hey, guys, why ya laughin?"

Arrogance or Resourcefulness?

Some woman wrote a book about spending a year in a women's prison for drug running, something about orange and black. She was a young, upper-middle class, well-educated white woman. Somebody gave her a crappy one-star book review, saying she appeared to be condescending and arrogant. This was, in part, for claiming that while she was in prison, she was able to get along with everyone and was everyone's friend. The book claimed that she accomplished this by helping others, often falling back on her education—maybe helping with legal work, for example.

Well, remember how I spoke about the importance of finding your niche in prison? What this woman did was just that. To call that arrogant *is* arrogant. First of all, few people behind bars have a college education, so there is a much higher premium on educated help and advice in prison than there is on the outside.

In addition, the majority of detainees and inmates I met along the way were represented by public defenders because they couldn't afford attorneys. Nothing personal, but for the most part, relying on a public defender to go out of his or her way to help you is often a miserable proposition. When you're behind bars, you need all the help you can get, and believe it or not, sometimes a shrewd, well-educated inmate can actually offer better advice than a deadbeat PD.

Second, if it works for you, if it helps you to survive, you do it. There were guys who had nothing to offer but a serious beatdown, and they used it to push people around because that's all they had. Some of these guys ended up in groups and gangs where intimidation was their game. Others always managed to have money for commissary, and they used merchandise to pay people off. And let's not forget the guys who were expert at mouthing high-demand medications, which were used to wheel and deal for what they wanted.

The bottom line is that education is a commodity, and just like any other gift or attribute, there is a value attached to it—and in prison that value is quite high. You've got to leverage your power.

Remember, prison is a microcosm of society, a bubble, a vacuum, or whatever you choose to call it, but there is still a nexus between the free world and the world of incarceration. What I mean is that all of us use our assets to attain and maintain goals and relationships, and arrogance has nothing to do with it.

Here's a closing thought. I once read this quote by Rick Castro: "The higher up you go, the more gently you have to reach down to help other people succeed." It's just a fact.

Tipping the Scale?

In the county jail, non–US-citizen detainees seemed to get far better accommodations and humane treatment than we did. Some shithead CO once tried to tell me it was because they weren't all there for criminal activity and were just being held in custody until further notice. Sorry, but that's just bullshit! Half the guys on my tier were awaiting trial and were therefore not legally guilty of anything because they hadn't even been convicted and sentenced yet.

More likely, the more "humane treatment" was because the county facility is compelled to follow federal government guidelines for non-US-citizens. With direct federal oversight, the local-yokels had to watch their asses and actually *follow* the rules. For us local boys, they could bend the rules to suit themselves. Anyway, these noncitizen detainees were isolated from the rest of us and received more perks and fewer restrictions than we US citizens—perks such as reasonable access to computers, contact visits, and less restrictive telephone use, just to name a few. Don't get me wrong—I didn't have anything personal against these guys, just the system itself. My two biggest gripes were the expensive and convoluted process for setting up a phone account and making a lousy phone call and the no-contact-visit policy for us Americans.

First, let's talk about the phone. Yes, there are phones available for prisoner use. In the facilities I "visited," there seemed to be about three phones per fifty inmates. Yes, you are allowed access to these phones during rec time and tier time. That sounds wonderful, right? Wrong!

You can hardly do a damned thing with a jail phone without first having someone from the outside open a special account for you. Accounts are opened with private entities such as Global Tel Link and others who offer a local calling rate of about twenty-five cents a minute. These accounts must be opened by your friend or relative on the outside, and they must pay a processing fee, load the account up with money, and then maintain a running balance that is gradually etched away as you make your phone calls—just like one of those prepaid credit cards or a debit card. If you had no one on the outside willing and able to set up an account for you, you were out of luck—and many guys fell into this category. We were given ten minutes per call, after which time we were promptly disconnected. Just as an aside, a detainee's phone calls are not private. The authorities can eavesdrop or record your conversations at will.

So what's my issue with the phone-call process? For me, it was the limited time allotted per call and the cost. Besides prisoners and assholes, who the hell pays twenty-five cents a minute plus fees to make a local call? Still worse is the fact that you're limited to ten minutes. The facility isn't paying for the freakin' call; you and your family are. And on top of that, you're paying through the nose. Limiting a detainee's phone time is meaningless and pompous.

Then there's the no-contact-visit rule. You've seen it on TV. You're on one side of the glass, and your visitor is on the other, and you speak through a phone receiver. It sucked big time. You know, I eventually got to the point where I could handle just about anything and everything that came with being locked up, but I despised the fucking authorities who wouldn't allow me to hug my wife and family when they visited. It used to kill me.

Visiting day was the most invigorating, exciting, and fulfilling event to look forward to in jail. There was nothing better. But it always turned out to be an emotional roller coaster because it hurt so much to have only twenty minutes to see your loved ones, and you had to do it behind a glass fucking window on a phone receiver. The only real reason for no-contact visits was the concern for drugs and contraband being brought into the facility. For guys like me whose charges had nothing to do with drugs whatsoever, there was no reason for such restrictions. How hard would it be to determine which offenders posed a drug-smuggling threat and which ones did not? It absolutely can be done, and state prison is my proof. Yes, we'll talk later about how well the state prison handled contact visits.

No more ranting and whining from me. Everything else was just peachy.

Telephone Wars

Yes, visiting day and phone calls were extremely important to me. I called either my wife or a family member on almost every break, and my wife was always there for me on visiting day. For the most part, there were no glitches, and I thanked God for being able to have that connection with the outside world. For me, this connection was a lifesaver.

That said, the phone situation could get really ugly at times and could cause some considerable problems. One of the biggest problems was called "tag teaming" the phones. Just as you would expect, if you wanted to make a call, you had to stand and wait in a line until one of the phones became free and then just step up to an available phone and make your call. This worked fine for most of us reasonable adults on the tier.

But then there were groups of mainly young guys who had to be running around like freakin' babies at all times and couldn't bear that they might have to stand in line to make a phone call like the rest of us did. So they would tag-team one or more of the phones. Tag-teaming meant when the first guy finished his call, he would stand there and hand off the phone to another guy who was off playing cards, watching TV, taking a shower, or doing whatever. Then that guy would do the same thing and hand the phone to the next guy, and the next. You get the picture. That meant that the rest of us guys had to stand there like assholes waiting for a chance at the phones—the whole while, watching the clock tick away and realizing we might not get to make our call at all before our rec time ended.

The COs wanted nothing to do with the tag-teaming issue. They didn't want much to do with anything on the tier that was for the benefit of the detainees. So once again, the guys who gave a damn about the tag-teaming problem had to get creative and work out our own solution.

Of course there was always plan A, which was to just kick the tag-teamers' asses, but that would most likely get you put in solitary. We put our heads together and came up with a nonconfrontational plan. This one was actually all mine. It was simple, and it was musical. We would sing! That's right—every time the tag-team assholes started to do their thing, we would gather around the phone they were on and sing as loudly as we could into their faces. Sometimes "Jingle Bells," sometimes a Beatles song, even "Mary Had a Little Lamb" would do the trick.

After a few confrontations and scuffles, the tag-team assholes gave up and waited in line to make their calls like the rest of us mindful individuals. Of all the songs we sang in the faces of the tag-team assholes, the favorite seemed to be the old 1980s song "867-5309/Jenny" by Tommy Tutone. Everybody knew that one.

Unlucky

There was this one guy who always stood out in the crowd. For whatever reason, he managed to grab everyone's attention and keep everyone guessing. That was Lucky. He was a tough little bastard, a local boy at the county facility. Although he was really just a big, goofball kid in a man's body, he was still intimidating enough to keep everyone around him on guard and a little off-kilter. This guy was nonstop, like the Energizer bunny with crooked teeth and a bad attitude.

Lucky had a cousin and an uncle on the same tier, and he had a sister and another cousin in the women's section of the same facility. The whole family had apparently been in and out of this jail facility throughout the years like a vacation home in the Hamptons. It might sound like I'm stating the obvious, but I came to recognize the guys who had spent lots of time in jail because they were the best at doing it. You could pick them out from the minute they arrived on the tier. They were the ones who seemed unaffected by the whole experience and had a knack for swiftly dominating and intimidating their way around without a hitch.

Those were also the guys who annoyed me so much at Rikers. Why? It just got on my nerves. When you're a responsible adult and you've got the weight of the world on your shoulders as you contemplate your upcoming prison sentence, it sucks having a bunch of smartass losers boogieing around like they're at the shopping mall or high-school gym class. No, I don't mean all of them, but many.

For whatever reason, Lucky wanted to be my friend. Maybe he needed a father figure in his life, or maybe it was the fact that I gave him "stuff" from my commissary like coffee, crackers, and other items I really didn't care much about because I felt bad for him. Like a lot of the guys, he had no one on the outside who would give him money for commissary. I had pictures of my kids in my cell. He was enamored with the picture of my twenty-four year old daughter. Of course this really annoyed me at first, and I was constantly kicking his skeevy ass out of my cell for staring at the photo of her.

Then one day, I walked into my cell from the shower and caught him staring at the picture again. When I grabbed his shoulder to spin him around and throw him the fuck out of my cell, I saw that he was crying. He was standing there like a big baby with tears in his eyes, which he denied, of course. I was a bit stunned and asked, "What the hell is wrong with you?"

He started rambling on about how he "never had a real family, just wanted to be like everyone else," and how he wished he could marry a girl like my daughter.

I stopped him there. *Oh, geez, what the fuck do I do with this?* I asked myself. Do I pat this psycho kid on the head and tell him everything is gonna be OK? Do I tell him to fuck off and throw his ass out of my cell?

Well, I kinda did both. I gave him some of that good old fatherly advice and told him he had a long life ahead of him and that someday he would marry someone and have a family of his own. I told him he'd have to act right and get a job and prove himself as a good, responsible, and caring man—and then I threw him the hell out of my cell with a warning that he'd never get another commissary item from me again if I caught him looking at my pictures.

The irony of all this was that I didn't believe a word of what I told him. He was so fucked up in the head that his chances of ever dealing with the outside world and making a real life for himself seemed slim to none. I'm sorry, but it's pretty fucking hard to grow apples on an orange tree.

Months later, my notions were confirmed when I heard through the grapevine that his charges jumped up from credit-card fraud to first-degree murder. He was going to state prison for a long, long time. Keep dreaming about that "family," Lucky. It's probably the best dream you'll ever have.

The Farce That It Is

I'm going to go a little off the reservation on this one, so please humor me. This is one of my personal pet peeves.

Environmentalists would absolutely cringe at how much water is wasted in jails and prisons. It shouldn't surprise anyone that water consumption might be high in these facilities, but here's a situation that goes beyond the pale of high consumption and is, in fact, just plain old irresponsible—better yet, inexcusable.

First, let me just say that detainees take first place on the list of abusers, and there is absolutely no concern for water conservation on their part. Endless and totally unnecessary toilet flushing and water running in the sink is the norm, and this is perpetuated by detainees with reckless abandon. Yet, for a detainee this is not so surprising.

You could easily argue that the last thing an inmate is likely to have on his mind is water conservation because the basic essentials of life such as eating, sleeping, and self-preservation take precedence over all else. However, there is absolutely no excuse for the officials who run these facilities. For them to ignore and outright abuse the conservation of water is absolutely inexcusable. When it comes to practical, commonsense approaches to maintaining highly populated facilities, the expectation is that public officials should be held accountable for the decisions and actions they take in doing so. It's maintenance 101, right? Appropriate action should be taken when a maintenance problem arises. Well, then, why shouldn't water and simple plumbing maintenance be dealt with appropriately? Not to mention the fact that there is always a price to pay for a lack of action.

By now you're asking, "Where is he going with this, and why the hell is he talking about plumbing? Who gives a shit?" The answer is simple. I want to illustrate the complete lack of logic, concern, and responsibility that sometimes exists on the part of those whom we trust most—those we expect to be "responsible" and to do the right thing. The supposed "pillars of justice" are, in this instance, the overseers of our jail and prison facilities.

Having lots of time on your hands as you waste away in jail, you find ways of staying busy. That's why I decided to work out a little calculation, which illustrates the outrageous waste of resources I witnessed day in and day out at the county facility. I counted the amount of days, the number of gallons, and the associated cost incurred by the senseless waste of water and sheer lack of concern by the administration. Here we go.

I once watched a shower remain running twenty-four hours a day for thirty-four days straight before it was finally repaired. I watched a sink run full blast for fifty-seven days before it was only partially repaired. I watched a toilet run for sixty-two days before a plumber was called in to repair it. To keep it fairly simple, I'll stop there, but believe me, this was just the tip of the iceberg. To make my case, I'll focus on just these three particular incidents and illustrate the complete lack of regard on the part of law-enforcement officials at the county facility.

- The Shower Equation: To take a fifteen-minute shower every day, the average person uses 915 gallons of water in a month. With the shower running twenty-four hours straight, and assuming you could take four fifteen-minute showers in an hour, that's ninety-six showers. Now, ninety-six showers @ 915 gallons per shower = 87,840 gallons of water use per day. So, 87,840 gallons x 34 days = 2,986,560 gallons of water wasted.
- The Sink Equation: With a faucet running full blast, you waste about forty-eight gallons of water an hour. So forty-eight gallons per hour x 24 hours in a day = 1,152 gallons per day. Now, 1,152 gallons x 57 days = 65,664 gallons of water wasted.
- The Toilet Equation: A toilet running all day uses about 150 gallons of water a day. So, 150 gallons x 62 days = 9,300 gallons of water wasted.

Therefore, not even considering sewer costs, which are based on the amount of the outward flow of water down the drain, and not even considering other incidents beyond these "tip of the iceberg" examples I've given, here is the consequential damage and the associated cost according to US Geological Survey and Environmental Protection Agency standards:

- A total of 3,061,524 gallons of water was wasted due to the negligence of the facility. At a US average cost of $2.00 per 1,000 gallons of water, that's about $3,062.[3] Now, in a facility of six tiers, we would have to assume they were experiencing similar water issues.
- So that's $3,062 x 6 tiers, which amounts to $18,372 of your tax dollars going straight down the drain in a two-month period. Who

---

3 "Water Science Activities—Drip Calculator: How Much Water Does a Leaking Faucet Waste?" US Geological Survey website, http://water.usgs.gov/edu/sc4.html.

the hell knows why? To avoid a $500 plumbing bill? One can only guess.

It's hard to even fathom what those figures would be if a detainee's personal water abuse, sewer costs, and all of the other incidences of water waste were included in the equation. Then consider that this waste and abuse is happening at thousands of other correctional facilities throughout the country, 24/7. The numbers are astronomical. It boggles the mind.

So what's my point? Simply this: accountability cuts both ways. Our expectation of detainees and inmates is that they should be held accountable for their actions, and that's why they ended up incarcerated. Well, then, so should those who run our jails and prison facilities be held accountable when they are blatantly negligent and disrespectful to our natural resources and taxpayers. Things like the IRS scandal, the Veterans Administration scandal, and other governmental blunders and waste come to mind. Come on now, the government should be held fully accountable just like the rest of us. That's all.

Oh, and one last thing. Remember the shower that ran for thirty-four days straight? Well, it was only the hot water that was working. Without any cold water to add to the mix, the shower water was literally scalding hot. I mean dangerously hot. Very few of us on the tier even attempted to use the shower during that period of time, which makes for a whole cluster of interesting and pungent hygiene issues, but that's not even the point. This shower water was actually hot enough to blister your skin if you were stupid enough to dive right in—and a few guys were, and did. Quite a few guys were walking around with red blotches and burns on their bodies. I was able to deal with it by taking a towel into the shower, wetting it in the scalding water, letting it cool down a bit, and then squeezing the water over my body, which I did for thirty-four days straight. Nice, huh?

The New Kid on the Block

A new kid showed up on the tier. He was about twenty years old. You could tell immediately that he was scared shitless, and he tried hard to remain unnoticed. In the outside world, it's not too difficult to live your life in the background, under the wire, or incognito as a defense mechanism or to avoid confrontation. Sorry, kid, not in jail. There, it's inevitable—like a contest where the odds are measured, a strategy is established, and someone eventually steps up and challenges you. Everyone knows everything anyone does or says, or tries not to do or say, always.

It only took a day or so for this kid to be confronted. For the first week on the tier, while everyone was sitting at their tables and eating meals, this kid had to sit on the floor with his tray of food because no one would let him sit at a table. You see, there was a hierarchy of seating arrangements, and you had to earn your table and seat. Most guys managed to do this almost immediately, either schmoozing their way to a spot by befriending someone else at a particular table or making it known that they were willing to fight for their spot if anyone should choose to challenge them.

The new kid did neither. He tried a few times to sit at a table but was knocked down, tray and all. He just picked up what he could and went back to sit on the floor. The more that time went on, the worse this kid was being treated—the way animals pick at the weak and the wounded. It was really beginning to make me sick—and angry.

Let's digress for a minute. I managed to stay strong and focused throughout most of my journey, and for a nonviolent man in his early fifties, I was still able to develop a persona that was intimidating enough to keep the general population from messing with me. A few fist fights where you come out on top are usually enough to earn this status. And I did. But deep inside, I was not cut out for fighting and all the tough-guy bullshit. Not only was I too old, and wise, for that crap, but I didn't have the heart to watch some of the more timid guys being hammered by the psycho assholes on the tier who thrived on torturing the lost souls and weakhearted.

One day I just lost it. The new kid was once again sitting on the floor with his dinner tray. I got up from my table and walked over to him where he was crouched in the farthest corner of the tier, eating his dinner. I told him to get up and follow me. Hesitantly, he did. We walked back to the table where I sat, and I told him to sit down at an empty space next to me. He started to shake and almost dropped his tray of food, but he sat down at the table with me.

Then I said, "From now on, this is where you sit," loud enough for everyone on the tier to hear me. It was a big risk, and I wasn't sure if he or I would be challenged, but we weren't. I learned that his name was Andre. Over the next few weeks, things seemed to be getting better for him. He had befriended a few other young guys on the tier, and I moved on, never really having much to do with him again.

About a month went by, and my friends and I were hanging out at our usual spot during rec time. All of a sudden, there was insane screaming coming from the upstairs bathroom and a bunch of guys scrambling around and running to their cells. Andre was thrown into a scalding shower by his supposed "new friends." Every time he tried to get out of the scalding hot water, he was pushed back in. He was burned badly.

Why? It was because Andre decided to spill the beans about why he was in jail. It turns out that he was there on arson charges. Not just that, but rumor had it that there were kids in the house he torched, and they received third-degree burns and were permanently scarred. They were nearly killed in the incident.

A few guys always managed to get a newspaper onto the tier. We had all read about the horrendous arson incident in the newspaper a month earlier but never made the connection. It wasn't hard for me to reconcile between my initial compassion for "the new kid being hammered by the psycho assholes" and the heartless piece of shit who could burn and almost kill two innocent kids. My perspective was entirely turned.

I spoke to the guys who did this to Andre, and one of them blurted out a sarcastic little rap that started with, "Tit for tat, when you in jail, that's where it's at." Another guy just said, "You don't burn down houses with kids in them. The little psycho prick deserved it." Who could argue with that?

From that point forward, nobody wanted anything to do with Andre, so his life on the tier was a living hell. Back to square one for the new kid on the block.

Above the Fold

When the proverbial shit hits the royal fan, you find out quickly who your friends are. It's amazing. That old cliché about how everyone wants to be your best friend when you're on top of your game, but then drop your ass like a hot fucking potato when you're down, is so blatantly true. In fact, some will actually walk by and give you a few kicks in the teeth while you wallow in your demise. With few exceptions, this rang true for me.

It was the afternoon lull on the tier. Guys were just hanging around playing cards, watching the crappy little busted-up TV in the corner of the tier, passing around portions of the one and only two-day-old newspaper, staring out the window, or just doing a bunch of nothing.

Somebody across the tier from me yelled, "Hey, look at this!" I saw a bit of a scuffle and guys gathering around to look at something in the newspaper. "That's him. The old guy over there," he said, and I noticed the group of guys all turn to look at me. The group headed over to me with the newspaper, and one guy said, "You made front page...above the fold!"

To me, this really sucked, but to them it was a badge of honor. To me, reading the one-sided, chest-pounding rhetoric being quoted by the authorities and the lynch-mob frenzy that surrounded my case turned my stomach, but to the young guys on the tier, the higher the profile, the badder the dude. In any case, these guys actually taught me something. I'd never heard the term "above the fold," meaning front-page headline news, so it felt a little surreal having everyone gather around me as if it were some kind of rite of passage. There were many more articles to come. Yes, for a stretch, I was in the papers regularly, gradually making my way down to pages two and three.

Most of the articles were sensationalized and annoying for me to read. It wasn't enough for them to just state the facts. The powers that be just couldn't get over themselves for supposedly apprehending me, completely ignoring the part where I returned to the United States with the sole intention of turning myself in. As ridiculous as it seems, I was even touted by the prosecutor and placed right up there on the same pedestal with a guy at the same facility who was charged with first-degree murder and a list of other glaringly violent criminals. Hey, now, I guess they gotta earn them brownie points wherever they can get them.

In the midst of all of the overblown media attention about me and my charges, I wrestled with the feeling of isolation and abandonment as I struggled to deal with the fact that essentially no one ever stepped up to simply say, "Hey, he may be guilty of this crime, but I've known him for years, and he is a damned good man." Sadly, I waited for that day, that moment, that instance where I would read an article that might include just one fucking kind word, but nothing—and more nothing after that.

Eventually, I latched onto this bit of profundity written by Thomas Paine, which helped me come to terms with my anger and my heartache. He wrote, "Reputation is what men and women think of us; character is what God and angels know of us." Let me translate that into prison lingo: "God knows, and everyone else blows."

How about you? Are you one of those credulous people who think the bonds of true friendship can never be broken? Do you think or say things like, "Oh, not him, not her; they would never abandon me?" Guess again, sucker. You don't know jack shit about your friends until you become society's underdog, one of the accused, expelled, and incarcerated. Count all those true friends you think you have in your life right now, and cherish the moment.

Here are a few clichés for you: "Now is just a snapshot in time" or "Friends are like dust in the wind." Someone I used to know once said, "In the flash of a moment, they'll blow away like the clouds." He'd say, "Maybe you'll blow away the clouds, but you won't feel nothin' when I'm gone." Home, that is.

Anything for a Cold Drink

Crazy shit goes on in jail. Things that people wouldn't dream of doing on the outside somehow become acceptable in the chaotic world of incarceration.

In county jail, you get your three square meals a day, and if you have someone on the outside sending you a little money, you can order limited items from the commissary. The only means of heating your food is hot water because there is no heat source for heating coffee, soup, etc. So if hot water doesn't do it for you, you're out of luck, and the closest you're going to get is lukewarm.

In contrast, the closest thing to cold you will find is the cold water you get from the sink in your cell, so there is no way to keep things cold, either—except one. The water in the toilet maintains an exceptionally cold temperature, thanks to the hard, cold, stainless steel that these lovely prison-style toilet/sink combos are made of. Do you see where I'm going with this? Bingo! Many of the guys stored milk, juice, and other sealed containers submerged in the icy cold water of their toilets. They would toss these items in a sock or their fishnet laundry bag and hang them in the toilet.

For me and many others, the thought alone made us sick, and warm drinks were a much better option, but to many, this was the norm. It's amazing how being treated like a helpless creature in a cage can lower your standards and defy your common sense to the point that storing food containers in your toilet is considered acceptable.

Big Red's TV Mystery

"Once upon a time," fifty guys shared one television. It was located at the corner of tier L-105 at the county jail. You guessed it—control of the TV was always a confrontational and volatile issue. There were constant arguments and fights and sometimes even (drum roll, please) sabotage!

I didn't pay too much attention to TV, but a group of us used to like to watch reruns of shows like "The Sopranos," "Cops," and a few other daytime doozies. Most of the young guys used to like watching MTV or ultimate fighting and other sports programs. The black contingent watched a little of everything but mostly wanted to blast some rap station they managed to find. So, for the most part, this was the semiregular pattern on the tier.

But then came big "Red." He was a big black dude who, right out of nowhere, decided that he was king of the TV. He would sit about three feet in front of it and control the who, what, and when of the TV. Because this guy was a 285-pounder with a "don't fuck with me" reputation, none of us guys were brave enough to mess with him.

So, after we just couldn't stand it any longer, we tried to put plan A into action, which was to enlist the help of someone who was willing to kick his ass. Actually, most everything in jail started with plan A—an ass kicking—and then you moved on from there. Nine times out of ten, it worked. But there was a problem in this case: the only guys who were capable of taking him down were guys who didn't give a damn about the TV. So, no dice, for quite a few weeks, big Red was king of the TV.

At first, this was a real quandary, but eventually we were able to devise a plan B. It was a plan of sabotage. About six of us decided that if we couldn't watch TV, then he wasn't going to watch TV, either. We waited until count time was called, and everyone started to clear the tier. A few of us went to grab the COs' attention by bullshitting and complaining about the scalding shower water, while a few others lingered around the TV until the last possible second. One guy unplugged and ripped the power wire out of the back of the TV and shoved the disconnected end into an opening through the back of it. Another guy poured a few glasses of water into it through a top vent.

The next time big Red came back out to the tier, we all watched from the second floor as he tried everything he could think of to get that freakin' TV working. He shook it, pounded on it, and don't ask me why, turned it upside down. We were laughing uncontrollably and had to move out of sight so no one would figure out we had something to do with the TV dilemma—especially him. It actually took him a full ten minutes or so to figure out that the power wire had been ripped loose. He was pissed! He was jumping up and down and yelling across the tier, "I'm gonna kill the motherfucker who messed with 'my' TV."

Within about twenty-four hours, some other genius figured out how to reconnect the power wire. Big Red was right there ready to pounce on the TV as soon as that wire was repaired. But, remember, they didn't know that not only was the power wire broken, but water had been poured into the TV, too. When big Red turned it on, the TV started humming, sparking, and smoking until there came a huge "bang," and it was dead. It was a sight to see.

The six of us guys who planned this sweet sabotage were proud as hell of our accomplishment. In jail, it's the little things that count. The whole tier was put in lockdown for the next twenty-four hours, and we no longer had a TV on the tier, but it was well worth it. Big Red was king of nothing but his own dirty underwear. "The kingdom had been overthrown, and all the orange-jumpsuit minions rejoiced in contentment and joy."

Angels without Wings II

Being in jail for extended periods of time has a way of rattling your brain and recalibrating your mind-set. It's a by-product of being forced into survival mode. Everyone reacts differently, but we all search for and ultimately latch onto that sweet spot or that comfort zone that helps us maintain our sanity. It's just human nature.

Some of the hardest times in jail are the silent, lingering hours you spend in the humble confines of your cell. For me, it was that relatively quiet time after the nightly ten o'clock lights-out announcement over the loudspeakers, commonly known as count time. You're lying there staring at the concrete ceiling and contemplating life, recounting the error of your ways, and missing your family so bad that it hurts you to the bone. I'm talking about a pain and longing that most people will never have to endure and one that I hope I will never feel again.

In times like these, people naturally grasp for some peace of mind, some solace and consolation. Unfortunately, having been out of touch with my Christian roots during this disastrous period of my life, I struggled with the notion of just "giving it to God," which had always saved me in the past. I did try, but the guilt, the anxiety, the explosive jailhouse environment, and the sheer insanity of my predicament made it extremely difficult to align with my spiritual side. It was just way too chaotic.

But as time went on, one thing kept flashing through my mind throughout the months leading up to my ultimate release from incarceration: the woman I met on the airplane while returning to the United States many months earlier. Her face, her words, and her voice used to echo through my head, providing me with a feeling of gratifying calm and composure. The only way I could describe it was "angelic."

Now, I'm a pretty practical guy, and it's not like me to focus on such things, but I began to think of her as my "angel without wings." I had never felt such a presence before, nor have I felt one since, but this was an amazing feeling that I cherished and looked forward to in those quiet, sad, and all-too-miserable hours after "lights out" was called over the loudspeakers.

Angels without Wings II

There are people led astray
There are those who'll take your life and walk away
And there are those who sit and wait for judgment day—yes, there are those who sit and wait for judgment day

Now, the spirit in me sings
Look no further, you're the soul of many things
And I still believe in angels without wings—yes I still believe in angels without wings

Who's gonna listen to you when you call
Who's gonna catch you when you start to fall
Who's never gonna make you sit and wait
Who's gonna open up heaven's gate
The time has come to make your choice
Will you listen, when you hear the voice of an angel without wings?

Chef Ramen and the Honey Bun Express

Food in the county jail was as bad as you might imagine. Try to imagine the worst, most bland cafeteria food you've ever had, and then add lots of water. That will give you a good idea of what we're talking about here. Yes, everything was floating in a quarter inch of water, probably because everything was frozen and didn't get thawed before it was fried, baked, or who knows what. There was never a single item that was fresh on the tray, not even a lousy piece of fruit. Literally everything was frozen or came out of a can or box.

But, you know, it's all relative. There were some guys who actually didn't mind the food and were as happy as a clam with the crap we were served. If you ate shit food on the outside, then I suppose jail food would just be more of the same, and that seemed to be the case for at least half the guys on the tier. It's hard for me to fathom, but there is a whole world of people out there who place food and eating last on their priority list. Not at all true for me. Just ask my appetite and my gut. Yes, there were many of us who had a much deeper appreciation for eating well. We ventured to expand our culinary horizons and were determined to come up with other ideas and options. We got pretty creative.

Surprisingly, by combining some of the not-so-disgusting cafeteria items with our commissary items, we were able to conjure up some halfway decent things to eat. A group of about eight of us had a little nightly potluck gathering where we would indulge in the dish of the day.

I was the designated chef. If you wanted to be in our potluck group, a commitment was required. You had to contribute certain items from your commissary and dinner tray. If you didn't, you were out. No contribution, no food.

So here's a quick example of what I'm calling "halfway decent." One of the big favorites was what I called the "super seven burrito," which stood for our tier number and the number of ingredients in the burrito. From the commissary, I was able to get tortillas, Ramen noodles, barbecued corn chips, beef sticks, packets of mayonnaise and mustard, and the cheese packet from a package of macaroni and cheese. Of course, there were no utensils other than plastic sporks and knifes, so all of these items were crushed or chopped appropriately and then mixed with hot water in an empty corn-chip bag, shaken profusely, and steeped for about ten minutes until creamy.

This tasty mixture was then placed on your tortilla and rolled into a surprisingly pleasant little burrito that everyone on the tier was envious of. If we really wanted to splurge, the eight of us would agree to save a piece of our frozen meatloaf, hamburger, hot dog, or frozen chicken from dinner and add it to our burrito mix.

Then there was dessert. How about a fudge brownie, cornbread, peanut butter cake with a melted milk chocolate candy-bar syrup? Or a honey bun, cream cheese, and sunflower nut cake? You might think this sounds insane, but if you really want something badly enough, you'll find a way to make it happen. A little goes a long way in jail, so every tiny morsel of added pleasure is highly appreciated and embraced with gusto.

Hey, have you ever had a cornbread layer cake with peanut butter, cream cheese, and grape jelly filling? You don't know what you're missing.

The Day of Reckoning

Going to trial did not make sense in my case. With a few exceptions, I wasn't denying that I was guilty of the charges being brought against me, so there was little to argue about in a courtroom. Therefore, a plea deal made the most sense. The plea offer was simple: plead guilty to one charge and accept a five-year sentence in state prison.

I was of the opinion that a three- or four-year sentence would be fair and reasonable and did not like the idea of five. You see, by this point in time, I had become well versed in the sentencing process and, more specifically, in the state's parole eligibility requirements. I knew that a five-year sentence would imply a much longer wait time before I would be eligible for release on parole. In addition, after receiving a copy of my discovery package, which is basically a snapshot of the evidence the opposing party intends to use against you, I was excited to tell my attorney that many of my charges could be disputed or justified—almost two-thirds of them.

He was completely unimpressed and said, "Sorry, bud. Even if only one of these charges is real, you face the same outcome in terms of sentencing. Let's not waste our time."

After a few rounds of bullshit between my attorney and the prosecutor, it was settled. I would plead guilty to just one of the many charges levied against me. This came across better in theory and on paper but really meant nothing in terms of sentencing. It was five years just the same.

And so the infamous day of reckoning fell upon me. It was my long-awaited sentencing day. All of the anticipation and speculation preceding that moment seemed pointless as I was cuffed, placed in waist irons and leg irons, and shuffled in and out of the courtroom in about ten minutes. It was about as anticlimactic as a wet firecracker. Except for the part where I had to sign the plea agreement. With handcuffs attached to waist irons, I was left with about six inches to work with. I noticed a stupid grin on the face of the court clerk and court officer as I struggled to lean over the edge of the desk to write my signature, dropping the pen four times in the process.

Now, I'd finally become more than just a detainee. I had left my cell that morning as a mere jailhouse detainee and returned to my cell as a guilty man, a condemned man, a convict.

DONATO ALFREDANO

Write My Book for Me

I met Lonnie at county after the infamous Kool-Aid war. That was the time I grabbed the pitcher of Kool-Aid from the black lunch table in an effort to settle the ridiculous yet agonizing battle over who got the extra pitcher of Kool-Aid at dinner time. Lonnie was the guy who watched that event unfold and then nodded in approval of my actions. He was a black guy in his late thirties. Although I had seen him on the tier, I'd never spoken to him before the day he approached me to tell me what a brave soul I was to stand up and stake claim to "equal Kool-Aid rights." He hung out with the resident black crowd, who, for the most part, stuck to themselves.

When we started talking, we found out we had something in common: Rikers Island. I knew Rikers from my recent jaunt through the New York criminal justice system. He knew it from spending half his life in and out of there. He amazed me when he would tell me how great it was for him at Rikers and how he wished he could go back there rather than stay at the county facility we were in. My brief stint at Rikers was certainly memorable, but only in the worst of ways. Everybody's ride is different. I guess it's who and what you're most familiar with that makes a place feel like home.

Mainly for him, it was tough for us to spend much time hanging around on the tier without running the risk of aggravating the relatively moderate but ever-present black-and-white divide. Lonnie amazed me. Considering the kind of life he had led, which was filled with abuse, neglect, and crime, he had a way about him that was remarkably peaceful, pleasant, and friendly. He was calm and endearing in a way that commanded a lot of respect from those around him. This was a refreshing and extremely unique quality that stood out among all those on the tier, both black and white.

He let me know that he had a lot of respect for me as well. I wasn't sure whether to take it as a compliment or insult when he said, "Man, you're cool like the OG," which stood for the "original gangster" dudes. "They lived by the code," he said, referring to some of the gang leaders he'd met in prison in upstate New York over the years who still lived by the so-called convict code. These days, this code is less prominent and has been overrun by a new, younger crowd with more of an "every man for himself" attitude, according to Lonnie.

He often told me that both the black and the white contingent on the tier agreed I was a generous and righteous man. Only half serious, I tried to explain that the term "righteous felon" was oxymoronic, to no avail. I was flattered just the same.

As I got to know him better, Lonnie asked me if I would help him write a book, a memoir of his life on the streets of New York. I hesitantly agreed, thinking the task was going to be a pain in the ass. As much as I really respected this guy, I was already up to my ears with helping other detainees with their letters and legal work.

And so it began. To start, Lonnie brought me about twenty pages to read. The plan was to have me read, correct, comment, and even rewrite his story for him, if necessary. Like so many others on the tier, his spelling and grammar were horrific—but not half as horrific as the story itself!

He gave me no forewarning about what I was about to read. I was shocked, excited, and saddened all at once by what I was reading. It was both disturbing and captivating at the same time. Lonnie was basically enlisted into the gang culture at ten years old and acted as a runner for the older guys who were out there blazing up the neighborhood like "new jack city." He witnessed his first drive-by shooting on his eleventh birthday; he was in the vehicle with the shooter. He watched a man get tied up in a basement and shot dead when he was just thirteen. He was raised in an environment full of drugs, guns, and violence, and this didn't change for him until he was in his late twenties.

I give him a lot of credit. As I read the pages of his "book," I could see his transition from a crazy, balls-to-the-walls gangbanger to the calm and controlled persona that he showed me every day on the tier. His story is a great one. It is a story of a man who managed to break away from and overcome the reality of gang violence and the stigma attached to it.

I could go into much more detail and tell you dozens more shocking and disturbing things about Lonnie's life experiences, but I'll let him write that book. What I do want to point out is that I learned something from this young guy. The cliché "against all odds" would be a huge understatement in describing Lonnie's ability to survive the rock-hard life he had led. What's even more amazing is that he managed to carry himself with a level of dignity and "righteousness" that is difficult to come by these days, inside or outside the walls of prison.

Lonnie removed all doubt about whether a man can overcome the worst of circumstances and become an excellent human being, regardless of his troubled home life, his horrific environment, or the color of his skin. I always thought of myself as resilient and strong in dealing with life's downfalls, especially the whole prison experience, but my inner strength and vitality were nothing compared to Lonnie's.

Every person who is incarcerated, whether they committed the crime or not, whether they have been sentenced or not, whether they are literate or not, all have one thing in common with those in the outside world: we can all respect good, old-fashioned human decency, dignity, and generosity. They are a man's most redeeming qualities and what matter most. That's right—the degree of culpability, speculative judgment emanating from others, cynical public opinion, and a tarnished reputation do not truly define a man. I'm going to say it again: it's what's in a man's soul that defines him, and only God truly knows what's in a man's soul. Don't judge.

I knew I would never forget Lonnie. The day I was shipped out of county jail and off to state prison, I held Lonnie's head between my two hands and kissed his forehead as I said good-bye. At that moment, off to the side of the tier, the black contingent all put their heads down, looked away uncomfortably, and pretended not to notice. The modest crowd of white guys who were standing next to me gleefully shouting out their good-byes slowly backed away, and for a brief moment, the room fell silent as I was escorted off the tier to make my trek to state prison.

CHAPTER 4
Real Men Wear Beige

State Prison

So I finally made the big time and arrived at state prison. The big D-O-C. Yep, I was now the sole property of the Department of Corrections. Arriving at the state prison is one of the most anxiety-producing and demeaning experiences a detainee will come to know. That's right. I was convicted, sentenced, and just earned a real nifty new title: convicted felon. Gee whiz, just like in the movies!

The grand entrance to state prison is one of the most humbling experiences and invokes some of the most haunting emotions you can imagine. Like an onion over a hot fire, I felt every layer of humanity being peeled away from me, as I was poked, prodded, and plopped into the caldron full of vermin and disdain known as prison—kinda like the waiting room in hell, I would imagine. Let me put it another way. I'd just come from county jail, and through intimidation and psychological manipulation, I was systematically being reduced to a nice, warm pile of subhuman protoplasm. If you were a first-timer, like I was, it was a feeling of being condemned to a world of uncertainty and the realm of the unknown.

Let's take it step by step. As is the case in many states, I was taken to an intake center where I could wait for days, weeks, or months before being assigned to a permanent resting place, which, according to my sentence, would be five long years—technically. Thank God for Parole.

The first thing I want to mention is pulling up to the facility and being in awe of the amount of barbed wire and chain-link fencing glistening before my eyes, like a row of twelve-foot Christmas trees—layer after layer of shiny stainless steel and barbed wire that was almost blinding to look at on this fine, sunny afternoon. It was surreal at best and nauseating at worst. There was an air of "we mean fucking business" about it that made me want to curl up and crawl in a hole.

As we drove through the gate and shuffled out of the county transport bus, I remember chanting my song, "The Concrete Is My Only Friend" over and over again under my breath, stopping just long enough to harken the prophetic words and visualize the angelic face of the woman on the airplane who tried to comfort and console me at the beginning of my journey, my angel without wings.

Humiliation was the flavor of the day. There were eight of us on that bus from the county jail. We stood there in the sunshine with our bright orange jumpsuits, leg irons, waist chains, and handcuffs (otherwise known as transport restraints) and waited to be prodded through the grand entrance into the facility. We entered the building and began to make our way toward humiliation lesson number one.

Here is where we were ordered to strip down for a full-body inspection. All eight of us lined up naked and bent over while we were systematically checked for contraband and assessed for gang-related tattoos or distinguishing scars. There were three guys who had tattoos all over their bodies that included a few swastikas, daggers, syringes, and other fun stuff. Then there was me with two tattoos: one of a rose with my first girlfriend's name on it and the other a lightning bolt.

Guess who got pulled aside and harassed about having a lightning bolt tattoo? Yep, it apparently resembled some gang-related symbol, and I was questioned for twenty minutes about my gang affiliation. What? Are you kidding me? Remember, I was a fifty-two-year-old Italian guy who committed a white-collar crime! I'm the guy you want to hassle about gang tattoos? Oh, well, enough said about that.

Humiliation lesson number two was a chance to sit on the "BOSS's" lap. The Body Orifice Security System is just a glorified X-ray machine. One naked body after the other, we were all ordered to sit on the BOSS and be checked for any internal contraband that might be stored in our bodily orifices. All I could think about was the slimy, sweaty feeling of sitting on that warm and damp plastic chair. It wasn't wiped down even once as about twenty different asses were parked there.

From there, we were taken to humiliation lesson number three. This was where we were hosed down in a chemical shower to remove any unwanted varmints like lice, fleas, or who knows what. We were told not to rub our eyes or put our hands in our mouths for twenty-four hours or we could get sick. As far as I know, no one did.

Then it was time to be awarded our new prison clothes. There was an inmate worker who stood outside of the showers in front of a wall full of beige garb. He would size you up by eye and hand you three pairs of pants, shirts, boxers, white socks, and a pair of slip-on sneakers. It didn't matter if you disagreed with his assessment of your size; you got what you got. This is where we handed in our orange jumpsuits from county jail, which up until that point we had been carrying around with us naked. Three of us stood there, and this young guy nicknamed "Blu" was stupid enough to ask if he could keep his orange jumpsuit. The inmate worker looked down at him with total disgust, and I'll never forget what he said: "Hey now, act your age. Orange is for "playas" boy. Real men wear beige!" I remember thinking, *Hmm, real men wear beige. That sounds like some kind of catch phrase or song.*

Between each humiliation lesson along the way came a degrading barrage of petty jeers and abuses from the COs as they badgered us and ordered us from one place to another. In and out of holding cells and processing areas for about four hours straight, until it was finally over.

The most popular word in the intake center was "motherfucker." It was articulated by COs and inmates alike in at least every other sentence. It was kind of like the joker in a deck of cards. It could be anything you wanted it to be, and I was amazed at the abundance of creative ways this word could be used. Just about anything could be "motherfucking"—from assholes to attitudes to boiled eggs.

DONATO ALFREDANO

Real Men Wear Beige

Once upon a time there lived three men in a cage
One man said to the other man hey now act your age,
No black, no white, no gray, no orange jumpsuit rage,
No misdemeanor, time to turn that page,

Now I'm a brand-new edition baby hot off the shelf
Don't get too close you just might burn yourself
No mama, no papa, no civil rights, no minimum wage
No prosecution, time to turn that page,

Real men, real men wear, real men wear beige
Boo hoo, little boy Blu, is all in a rage
Real men, real men wear, real men wear beige
Congratulations now you're coming of age

I know you didn't do it buddy neither did I
Nobody's guilty we're just here for the ride
Now watch your back, don't take no flack, no busting a gauge
No persecution, time to turn that page

No parsley, sage, rosemary, just a whole lot of time
Let me introduce you to a friend of mine
I'm telling you once, I'm telling you twice, get up on the stage
No hesitating boy you're coming of age.

The Revelation

Wow, so there I was in my state prison cell. What a different world it was than county jail. After a few days in the state facility, I came to realize how its grandiosity was both intimidating and impressive at the same time. Believe it or not, I mean this in a positive way. After that mind-boggling grand entrance and intimidation routine I went through when I arrived, things started to fall into place, and I began to realize there might actually be a light at the end of this dark tunnel.

Unlike county jail, things seemed to happen fast and for a reason, like a finely tuned machine. Yes, even from the inside of a prison cell, the amazing display of organization, symmetry, and—dare I say it—respect oozing from the COs to the inmates was impressive and reassuring. You didn't hear much of that cocky, bullshit attitude the county COs displayed so abundantly. I was truly impressed by this change in methodology and routine, but something even more remarkable began to occur.

Something that had constantly annoyed me up until this point in my journey and made all the difference in the world to me: individualism! That's right. For the very first time in my journey, I felt as if someone actually read my file, realized why I was there, and made a serious effort to handle my case and categorize me appropriately. In other words, for the first time, a conscious and deliberate attempt was being made to place me with individuals of comparable criminal stature and where a white-collar, nonviolent, first-time offending fifty-two-year-old guy belonged.

Yes, after a short stint in what we'll call the state prison assignment center, I was sent to my final resting place—a small minimum-security facility with other regular guys. For all intents and purposes, it was a Department of Corrections work camp. There were doctors, lawyers, engineers, and others who fell from grace and were paying the price for the error of their ways. Wow, real people with real lives and real perspectives, and they don't all want to beat, fuck, or kill you. Hallelujah!

Here's how it worked. At the assignment center, inmates are called to a hearing where their case files are reviewed to determine where they will be sent for the rest of their sentence. What I experienced at my hearing was pretty amazing and illustrates the vast difference in attitude between the county jail system and the state DOC. I sat there quietly in a little wooden chair in the middle of a large hearing room, facing a panel of about five men and a woman, and I watched as the panel whispered back and forth and flipped through my file folder over and over again. One guy even looked underneath it, seemingly expecting there to be more.

This went on for what seemed an eternity to me but was probably about three minutes. They had their hands cupped over their microphones as they continued to whisper to each other with perplexed looks on their faces. Finally, one guy took his hand off his microphone, looked up at me, and asked, "You got five years for this?"

"Yes, sir," I said.

Another guy asked, "What else did you do, or, uh, is this your first offense?"

"Yes, sir," I said.

Then another asked, "And you're how old? Fifty-two?"

"Yes, sir."

Then just one more time for good luck, the first guy asked, "So, it says here you got five years for this 'official misconduct,' and if I have it right, that misconduct was actually based on you cheating on your expenses, right?"

I overheard him as he then smiled, partially covered his microphone, and mumbled to the guy next to him, "He must have had a pretty bad lawyer."

Even I cracked a smile at this wisecrack. Finally, after another minute of whispers and mumbling, the woman panel member looked up and said, "OK, all set. Looks like you just won the lottery, my friend. We're sending you to the 'crème de la crème.' It's a minimum-security facility for guys just like you. Consider yourself very lucky... oh, and act accordingly"

Forty-eight hours later, I was on the DOC bus to my new home. Wow, at this point in time, I was overwhelmed by the long-overdue barrage of rhyme and reason bestowed upon me. In reality, nothing could feel as good as my ride out of Rikers Island, but this ran a close second. Man, had I come a long way from Rikers Island to a minimum-security facility.

As I left the hearing room and walked from my chair past the next guy in line for his hearing, he blurted out to me, "What? It ain't even called prison no more old man, you goin' to a minimum security *fa-cil-it-tee!*" Yeah, it felt a bit like heading toward paradise. Well, not really, but after the jailhouse merry-go-round I just jumped off, even a trumped-up paradise was bliss. I felt another song coming on. Quick, get me a pencil!

A Trumped-Up Paradise

Gone are the days of rage and ruin
Now everybody's singing to a different tune
It feels like Christmas but it's only June
Who's eating pudding from a silver spoon

So why ya crying with your head in the sand
Not everything is gonna go the way you planned
But a bird in the bush is like two in the hand
You finally made it to the promised land

Why you searching for clues where crime don't have no face?
You know, love ain't got no business in this kind of place
You take the Bull by the horns and the Tiger by the tail
You keep your eyes on the prize and you ain't never gonna fail

Behold the wonderland before your eyes, now you're living in a trumped-up paradise
Ask me no questions and I'll tell you no lies, now you're living in a trumped-up paradise

God Bless Them Ever-Loving Contact Visits

Here's another great big hunk of that DOC common sense and much-appreciated liberation I've been talking about. Contact visits! Thank you, God. I was more excited than a kid on Christmas as I anticipated my first contact visit with my wife. Yes, I'll say it again. The simple things in life become so vivid and meaningful when they've been abruptly ripped away from you. Your perspective gets its ass kicked right the fuck into focus. That's for sure.

I wanted nothing more than to hold my wife in my arms, kiss her face, and feel close to her again. Unlike the county jail, we didn't have to communicate over telephone receivers with three layers of safety glass between us, and instead of twenty minutes, we were given a full two hours per visit.

There were no conjugal visits like you see in the movies and on TV. No, not a part of my DOC reality. But I was as grateful as grateful can be for those contact visits. Surprisingly, I came to realize that I was in the minority as far as this gratefulness and excitement over contact visits was concerned. Sure, with a few exceptions, everyone seemed to enjoy them and look forward to them, but I practically worshipped them. That's because my mind was just as much on the outside world as it was on the inside. I had ideas and plans in my head of what I was going to do on the outside, where I was going to go, and whom I was going to see.

During our visits, my wife and I were able to share stories of events and plan all the things we were going to do together when I was released. These were the things that helped me cope, kept me positive, and gave me a sense of purpose. Contact visits were the closest I could come to being home. Yes, they were truly my salvation.

This brings up an interesting point about the way everyone has their own way of dealing with incarceration and stress in general. I focused on the outside world and the future. Other guys were just the opposite, especially the younger ones. They focused on the inside world and the present. Was it an age thing? Maybe, but I think it was a bit more complex than that.

I believe it had more to do with what your life was like on the outside compared to your life in prison. It's all relative. If your life was crap on the outside, then it makes sense to assume the transition to prison life would be easier for you. I also think it had to do with what might be awaiting you on the outside. If you've got nothing to look forward to, then it makes sense to assume you aren't going to spend a lot of time looking forward. The guys focusing on the inside—let's just call them the insiders—seemed to be the same ones immersed in the daily jailhouse crap, too. On the neutral side, they were super focused on the daily crap like nonstop smoking and playing checkers, chess, and cards whenever possible. On the negative side, some focused on things like fighting, scamming, and intimidating.

To me, the jailhouse crap, as I call it, was something I would partake in only by necessity, and as I've said before, sometimes it does become a necessity. You're not going to just skirt around with a big smile on your face and expect to avoid confrontation. That works only in the free world. But here's the thing. The true insider chooses to build his day-to-day life, his existence, around the prison environment.

While I was there, it aggravated me to think that these guys were settling for, or giving in to, prison life. But I have now come to realize that we are all victims of circumstance, and we all have to carve our own path, so if your future is dark or dim, then the here and now is all you've really got. In any case, thank God for visiting days.

I Found a Comb

It was visiting day! Once again, I couldn't wait. At 8:00 a.m., full of the usual anxiety and anticipation, I stared out the window of the barracks, watching to see if I could spot my wife driving into the parking lot. An hour later, about thirty of us were being shuffled into the visiting area to see our family and friends. As you enter, you are searched from head to toe and then allowed to go to the seating area. You are allowed a quick kiss on the cheek and a short hug. No mouth-to-mouth kissing allowed. You would then sit in a chair opposite your visitor for the duration of your visit.

The biggest concern of the facility was contraband being sneaked in or out, and that's why no kissing or touching was allowed. Beforehand, the room was completely searched and cleared of absolutely everything but the chairs we sat on during visits. We were frisked on the way in to visits and strip-searched on our way out. There would be serious consequences if we were found with anything whatsoever on our bodies.

On this fine Saturday morning of visiting day, as I got ready to sit in the chair in front of my wife, I noticed a comb on the floor directly under my chair. It was one of those big plastic pic combs. I was immediately fearful that I might be accused of trying to sneak the fucking comb in or out of the visiting room. After squirming around in my chair for a minute trying to decide what to do, I grabbed the comb and walked it up to the CO at the front of the room, handed him the comb, and told him it was under my chair. He didn't say anything to me, but he did give me a death stare and sent me back to my seat. Throughout the entire two visiting hours, he was staring at me. I wasn't sure what to think about the staring, but I soon found out.

Visiting time was over, and all visitors were cleared from the area. It was time for the strip-search routine. You had to strip down completely naked. First, you had to bend over so the CO could check to see if you were hiding anything in your ass. Then you'd turn around and shake out your underwear, turn your socks inside out and your sneakers upside down, and shake them out, too. I was used to the routine, so normally it was no big deal.

Not on this day. When it was my turn for the routine, the CO came to me, poked me in the chest hard enough to make me lose my balance, and said, "So you want to be a smartass, huh? You want to make me look bad in front of the sergeant, huh? I know you brought that comb in here to see if I would catch it. And then you came right up front so the sergeant could see you hand it back to me."

After another half dozen pokes to the chest and a shove against the wall, I was allowed to get dressed and leave. As I headed toward the visiting-area exit, the CO was barking at me, saying, "You're going to pay for your smartass bullshit." What the fuck? I was shocked and amazed. What a bad fucking decision that was. For the next three weekends, my new nemesis, "the paranoid CO," was assigned to visiting-area duty, and he harassed me after each visit.

Was there a lesson to be learned here? That's a tough question. I don't think I could have won this one either way. If I hadn't handed in the comb, he would have probably noticed it, and I'd have been busted anyway. Sometimes it just is what it is.

Keeping a Low Profile

Who is the model inmate? Well, it depends on whom you ask. To a CO, it's probably the guy who cowers at his every glance and never opens his mouth. You know, the guy who asks "How high?" when he's ordered to jump. To the majority of inmates, well, it would be just the opposite. To them, the model prisoner is the guy who can "hold his own," maintain a persona that lies somewhere between assertive and semi-aggressive on the belligerency gauge, and has the balls to either spit in your face, or "floor" you if you try to tell him how high to "jump."

In terms of overall survival in incarceration, I believe the model inmate should fall somewhere in the middle of these two conflicting perspectives. It's a delicate balance between staying out of trouble with the COs and commanding enough respect from fellow inmates to keep them from challenging you. Relationships are crucial to your survival. My motto for many of the new guys, especially the young ones, was to "keep a low profile."

As I've already mentioned, that doesn't mean you can just "hide in the cracks" or "blend into the woodwork" because that will just make you even more of a challenge or target. But you can't be the guy who's in everyone's face, either, unless you're ready, willing, and able to deal with the consequences. I'm talking about either getting your ass kicked by inmates who are bigger and badder than you are or getting your ass thrown into segregation by the COs and having additional "time" slapped onto your bid by the authorities.

It's like one of those reality shows. You can put a dozen people together in a super-competitive environment, apply extreme pressure to the situation, and watch the pieces fall into place. A hierarchy develops before your very eyes. Just like that physics analogy I mentioned previously, "One change is continually balanced by another to form a steady state." There you go.

And here's another way to look at it. Didn't your mama always tell you, "It's all about moderation"? Too much of anything, whether we're talking about attitudes or prunes, will get you into trouble. I once heard a guy in state prison say to a young newbie, "Hey now, you gotta watch your back and you can't take no flak from nobody. But you still gotta keep it under a hundred, kid. You can't be busting the gauge."

Another guy said, "You keep standing in everyone's face, and somebody's gonna swat you down like a butterfly, like a butterfly in the rain." I really loved that line—very profound, very rational. So I wrote this song:

DONATO ALFREDANO

A Butterfly in the Rain

*Hold your head up high and keep your fists clenched in a rage,
He's got a razor in his pocket and a viper in his cage,
Now the devil's got your number and he's calling out your name,
And he's about to take you down—just like a butterfly in the rain.*

*Don't you cry out loud, just make believe it isn't real,
He's got a tombstone for a heart and he's just trying to seal the deal,
Now the devil's got your number and he's calling out your name,
And he's about to take you down—just like a butterfly in the rain.*

*The vilest deeds like poison weeds bloom well in prison air,
It's only what is good in man that wastes and withers there, [by Oscar Wilde]
When the devil's got your number and he's calling out your name
Don't you let him take you down, like a butterfly in the rain.*

*Don't you even try to wash away that dirty stain,
Crying only serves to keep your mind off all the pain,
Now the devil's got your number and he's calling out your name,
And he's about to take you down—just like a butterfly in the rain*

Smelling Like a Rose

Louie and I used to work out together in the weight room at the state facility. He was a small-framed, middle-aged Hispanic guy who got a three-year sentence for drug possession. He was one of nicest guys I knew in the state facility. We spent about two hours a day in the weight room, and then we would walk the equivalent of four miles around the yard, stopping after each mile to do four sets of twenty-five push-ups. Yes, by this time in my incarceration journey, I was in the best shape of my life. I had lost about seventy pounds in a year's time, and even at fifty-two years old, I felt like I was unstoppable.

Now, there was this asshole who claimed to be an ex-state trooper. He was about thirty-five years old. He wouldn't say exactly why he was there, and the little he did say seemed to change regularly, giving us all little doubt that he was full of shit. He was just an arrogant asshole, and not many guys would even speak to him. He couldn't stand that Louie and I were so dedicated and focused on our exercise routine. I don't know if it was jealousy, envy, or just shear arrogance, but every day he would wait until Louie and I were walking past everyone out in the yard and take the opportunity to shout out a bunch of bullshit to make fun of us.

One day, he shouted out, "Hey, look at that. It's mister fucking universe and his sidekick, Juan Valdez!" And then he tried to trip Louie as we were walking by. It took everything I had in me to keep from punching him in the face, but I had a better idea. I really wanted to turn his whole smartass routine around on him.

Loud enough for everyone in the yard to hear, I stopped and yelled back at him, "OK, asshole. So you think you can do better? I'll bet you your dinner tray that I can do twice as many push-ups as you in sixty seconds. Come on, tough guy, right here, right now."

He hesitated at first, but all eyes were on him, and he couldn't really back down without looking like a total wimp. I had no doubt in my mind that I could beat him, so I made it even harder on him by taunting him and asking, "What's the matter, are you too much of a pussy to beat an old man like me? I'll tell you what. For two dinner trays, I'll bet you I hit thirty push-ups before you finish your first twenty."

He was red in the face, and the veins in his neck were bulging, but he finally got up off his bench, took his shirt off, and started doing some ridiculous bobbing and weaving boxing routine. Man, what an idiot! Guys in the yard slowly moved in to watch, and one of the COs actually came over and offered to time us with his wristwatch. I don't think he liked the "state trooper" asshole very much, either. "OK, here we go," the CO said. "At the count of five, gentlemen—one, two, three, four, five." We hit the dirt.

When I reached thirty push-ups, he was at eighteen. That was one dinner tray. At the sixty-second mark, I was at forty-eight, and he was struggling for thirty-six. That was two dinner trays. He was humiliated, embarrassed, pissed off, and defeated. He stood there silently, shaking his head and staring at the ground as dozens of insults were hurled his way. Then he stormed out of the yard and back to his quarters. Louie and

I never heard any bullshit from this prick again. He became a lot quieter in general from that point forward.

I didn't really give a shit about the dinner trays, and I never held him to the deal. I was satisfied with just shutting him the fuck up. To be honest about the whole thing, this guy might have been able to kick my ass in a general brawl. After all, he was about seventeen years younger, but there's one thing I learned well in prison, and that was to pick your battles. It's not always possible to do so, but in this case, it was, and I knew I would win.

Sometimes everything goes as planned. As for "mister universe and Juan Valdez," well, we came out smelling like a rose.

Breaking Rocks in the Hot Sun?

When I was a kid, radio and television instilled in me that vision of those chain-gang prisoners with their black-and-white-striped jail garb, swinging sledge hammers and "breaking rocks in the hot sun." Besides the jail square on the corner of a Monopoly board, that was all my mind could conjure up when someone said the word "prison."

But there I was, some forty years later, learning the ropes and experiencing the real thing. The good news is that I was beginning to feel that life was getting a little better as each day passed. I was beginning to meet more and more guys who were just straightforward, regular guys.

One of them was an attorney named Barry who was in for some kind of embezzlement. He helped me out quite a bit when I first arrived. He gave me pencils, paper, envelopes, and stamps so I could write to my family and let them know where I ended up and that I was OK. He also gave me some commissary items like food, deodorant, and soap.

But the best thing he gave me was the inside scoop on how things were run at state prison, how the schedules worked, and how to get a good job detail. Yes, everyone had to work at the state facility. No sitting around all day bullshitting or playing cards and checkers like county jail. Work came first, play came last, and I actually liked the idea of having something to do during the day, something to focus on. Not much of a surprise that my attorney friend worked in the law library. Another guy I met was involved in real estate on the outside. He was there on some kind of "theft by deception" charges. He ended up with a job in landscaping, mowing grass, trimming bushes, and raking leaves. According to Barry, this guy wanted to work in the law library but pissed off one of the COs, and, instead, he was first shanghaied over to road maintenance for months before he eventually made his way into a landscaping detail. Barry's point was that you had to play your cards right and know whom to schmooze.

Ironically, I was placed in the administrative office to work as a clerk, which was considered one of the best jobs you could have. That's because the clerks usually controlled the work details and could move inmates wherever they were needed, just like Barry had said. Generally, everyone was assigned to a permanent work detail, but clerks could move inmates around if they could dream up an excuse to do so. This gave them enormous power, and everyone was envious and a little intimidated by them.

But I hated the fucking position for a number of reasons. One, I didn't care for the other punk clerks I worked with who took complete advantage of the power they had by treating all their buddies to the good details and sticking others with the crap ones. Basically, if you weren't paying them with commissary or favors, you were on their radar screen for being screwed. These guys were all young and thrived on flexing their muscles, but I didn't like the whole power-play game. I just didn't have the mind-set for such bullshit and couldn't stand being in the middle of it.

Two, a clerk works alongside the COs. Even though the state COs were light-years better than the prick COs I'd come across during my New York journey and at county jail, when you worked among them, they still tended to treat you like a peon. Inmate or not, being treated like shit by some of these half-witted, egocentric COs didn't sit well with me at all.

Eventually, I asked the captain to allow me to transfer to another detail. He was shocked and said something like, "Are you kidding me? I've never had anyone ask to transfer out of clerk detail. What's your problem?" After a brief discussion, he gave me twenty-four hours to find another detail with an available opening and threatened he would place me wherever he felt like if I didn't. I would have no say in the matter. But I knew exactly where I wanted to go. I wanted to work in the greenhouse.

I had scoped out all of the work assignments available at the facility, and I knew the greenhouse was the place for me. One, you were completely out of the sight and supervision of the COs all day long. Two, the detail supervisor brewed fresh, store-bought coffee every morning, and I wouldn't have to drink the swill they served us at breakfast. Last but not least, I'd have access to the vegetable garden of tomatoes, peppers, and cucumbers, plus a fridge often stocked with yogurt and condiments that were otherwise completely unavailable to us. What more could a man need!

I ran over to the greenhouse detail supervisor and pleaded for a spot, and I got it. This was the best thing in the world I could have done. My frame of mind improved leaps and bounds in this new detail. I loved it. Sure, it was still prison, but I couldn't imagine a better way to "do it" than this. If there was a jail in heaven, this was it. It was peaceful, relaxing, and even informative. We were given access to textbooks and took quizzes on a variety of horticultural subjects, and I came to learn and appreciate gardening in a whole new way.

I used to sneak vegetables into my quarters and prepare them as a snack at night. Of course we had no knives, so I used the lid from a can of tuna as a knife to slice them. Then I used to squeeze packets of mustard, ketchup, mayonnaise, and any other condiments I could scrounge up to make various sauces and dressings to put on them. I had never loved and appreciated fresh vegetables so much in my life.

I've mentioned how all things are relative. Sayings like, "You don't know what you've got 'til it's gone" and "Absence makes the heart grow fonder" come to mind. Yes, it's the simplest things that you come to appreciate when the boundaries of everyday life become so controlled and limited as they do in prison.

Tricky Mickey

Mickey was another guy I knew at state. He was an Italian guy who worked in the kitchen. He was a chef on the outside, and a damned good one at that. He and I would have long conversations about the various dishes we loved to eat and prepare back home. He was the real chef; I was just a great food enthusiast and self-taught home cook.

Part of Mickey's job was to prepare meals for the facility staff like the COs and administrative officials. They had their own menus and food items and did not eat any of the crap we ate. For them, Mickey made things like spaghetti and meatballs, fried chicken, submarine sandwiches, and other tasty dishes that we inmates would kill for.

He would sometimes invite a few of us to meet him "behind the kitchen loading dock in fifteen minutes," where he would covertly bring a few plates of whatever he had prepared for the staff that day.

We'd have minutes to finish whatever he gave us and run back to our work details before getting caught and into huge trouble, but it was worth it. We were like high-school kids cutting class and misbehaving. It was actually kind of fun and exciting. Yeah, things started looking—and tasting—better every day, and I was thankful that the worst seemed to be behind me.

Attorneys

"Can't live with them, can't live without them." You know, when you're behind bars, it becomes easier to get angry with the people and events that happen on the outside. As you might imagine, losing all control and being unable to do anything much about anything in your life can be frustrating. You're sitting around contemplating all of the things that coulda-woulda-shoulda been done to help your case, and you're completely powerless to do anything about it.

This makes your attorney the perfect target for your frustration and anger because he's the one steering the ship... through a shit storm of your own making, of course. Ironically, being angry with one of the only people who's on your team seems a bit illogical, but you still end up pissed at him most of the time. That said, in spite of the daily frustration and anxiety I was feeling toward my attorney, I couldn't wait to speak with him or see him. I couldn't wait for him to visit the facility to discuss my case and any progress that was being made. I knew from the beginning I was destined to serve some jail time, but I was obsessed with making sure that everything possible was being done to keep it to a minimum. I wanted to know every detail.

With all of the things I may have thought or said about my attorney, the truth of the matter is that I really liked him. I've spoken of him sarcastically along the way, but he was a damned good attorney and a very compassionate, sincere, and extremely likable guy. On my day of release, I left the courtroom to meet my wife and attorney, who were standing outside the courtroom doors. Holding back a rush of tears, I hugged my wife for a long while. When I finally stepped away from my wife, my attorney reached out to shake my hand and said, "Welcome home, stranger." I saw the shocked look on his face as I grabbed his hand and pulled him toward me to hug him for almost as long as I had hugged my wife.

The Daily Double

Timmy was his name, and gambling was his game. Timmy was in for something completely unrelated to gambling, but gambling was actually his biggest problem. He was a man who had some serious cash to his name. It would drive me crazy to hear him tell me about his weekend outings to Las Vegas and Atlantic City, where he had the play money and the know-how to score tens of thousands of dollars and then lose it all before coming home Monday morning to an infuriated wife and family.

I don't know the first thing about the diversities of table games and gambling, so I was amazed at the money-making potential that existed for someone who really knew what they were doing like Timmy did. I was truly enlightened and learned more than I ever wanted to know about games and gambling. Up until then, all I really knew was what I'd seen on TV and in the movies. Slowly but surely, the wheels began to turn in my head. I just couldn't stop thinking about ways to harness the power of someone who had the play money and the knowledge to generate these huge sums of cash.

Of course, the other half of the "Timmy" equation is that we're talking about an addict, and that's something I did know about. It was clear that he had a gambling addiction and just couldn't walk away from the tables. Typically, when a gambling addict is ahead of the game, instead of walking away, the flames of the addiction are fueled even further as he burns away all the money he's earned before crashing down from the excitement and the "high." Yeah, just like cocaine.

Regardless, we made some big plans! After we were both released, we planned to go to the casinos together. As he would start to do his thing and build up a good lump of cash, I would take half of it and escape to an undisclosed location. Later we would meet. I would split half of the money with him, and he could do whatever he wanted with it—even go back and gamble it away, for all I cared at that point.

Fast-forward. I was released before Timmy. He got out a few months after I did, and we spoke a few times on the phone about our big plans for a quick money grab at the nearest available casino. The plan was thwarted when I found out that Timmy had been out only a few weeks before being sent to federal prison on new charges—five years, I think. Nope, I never heard from him again.

Dream On

Yeah, I know. Timmy's story sounds a bit naïve and presumptuous at the same time, but remarkably, when you're in prison, things just sound simple, planning seems less complicated, and prosperity appears more attainable. That great big world that exists outside of the prison walls becomes like the legendary land of endless possibilities and bliss. In a way, it's like you're a kid all over again. When you scrape off the vast and various layers of contamination and corrosion that have engulfed you throughout the years, sometimes there's nothing left but an open mind and an open heart. Yes, even for scumbags, criminals, and addicts.

It's a funny thing. Some call it scheming and scamming, some call it plotting and planning, and some may call it hoping and dreaming, but when you're sitting there every day, thinking about things to think about thinking about, the possibilities are endless. Once I got to the state facility and the general population was, let's just say, a little bit older, wiser, and more enlightened, I was able to befriend guys who had some great ideas and firm knowledge on many things, from lug nuts to brain surgery. It sure made for some interesting conversations when a pharmacist, a lawyer, a diesel mechanic, a drug dealer, and a used-car salesman got together in the yard to discuss world politics or fine dining.

On the outside, the playing field is vast, and we have the luxury of staying away from people, places, and things we don't like or have nothing in common with. When you're incarcerated, it's nothing but an equal playing field. Nobody is more significant than the other, no matter what or who you were on the outside, so you end up with some unlikely character associations. Like one big happy family of misfits and innovators.

It's a Beautiful Day in the Neighborhood

Bigotry is alive and well in prison. Your skin color and ethnic origin will play a heavy role in the "who, what, and where" of your daily life, but not in quite the same way as they do on the outside. Sure, you see the usual segments of society like the black, the white, the rich, the poor, the good, the bad, and the ugly. However, the walls of prison not only act as a barrier in preventing escape, they also act as a barrier in preventing physical and emotional dispersion. I've mentioned this concept before. Unlike life on the outside, you can't just pick up and move to a new neighborhood if you don't like your neighbors or leave the party and go home if you don't care for the company. This makes for a very interesting and unique brand of coexistence.

Sure, as a general rule, inmates become segmented and polarized just like people do on the outside. For many guys, being part of a gang or posse or crew was the only way they knew how to survive. That's common knowledge, but what I found interesting was the high number of exceptions to the general rule. For example, when physical and emotional dispersion are not an option, the most unlikely friendships and alliances begin to form. This is not just an observation on my part; it was my experience. Being best friends with a black man, a skinhead, or a gay man were experiences I never had on the outside, but during my incarceration, such friendships fell unpretentiously into place, and I was thankful for them.

No, I've never been a prejudiced man, but I must admit that the number of biracial, multicultural friendships and alliances stunned me at first. I just wasn't used to it. I was never in the military, but I suppose the camaraderie and closeness that exists among soldiers is comparable. In a similar way, they face a kind of "barrier" in terms of the battlefield, or even while in boot camp, for that matter. In such desperate times as living in prison, people depend on one another for support and survival. You know what they say: "We all hear better when we're in pain." Our minds and hearts are opened. As a result, benevolence and camaraderie can have a much lower threshold.

I thank God for those friends in prison who helped me through the most devastating time in my life. For the relatively short time we spent together, these friends were genuine, and I was fortunate to have them. But the sad conclusion is this: since the day I stepped foot out of those prison walls, I never saw any of them again. Yes, phone numbers were exchanged and promises made, but nobody kept them. It's sad and ironic at the same time, but although I often think of my prison buddies, I have no desire to see them again. There would be no purpose for me or for them. Again, I'm sure this is true for many soldiers leaving the military as well.

You see, the outside world, the real world, has a way of slowly drawing you back in. Prison days and prison ways quickly fade. The best of friends and relationships just cannot compete with the all-powerful, all-encompassing world full of options, diversities, and personal freedom.

Jamie, Don't Blame Me

Jamie was a strange dude with a strange way of looking at life. He was hot and cold about everything—the epitome of bipolar disorder. For everything good he had to say about someone or something, there always seemed to be a negative attached, and he would often obsess over it.

He was a bit of a loner, but he and I hit it off immediately because we were both particularly focused on the outside world, and, like me, he did not care much for the local entertainment or the clamor of prison culture. We both had kids back home and talked about our love and dedication to them. We would often sit together, apart from everyone else in the yard.

Aside from sharing pictures of our kids and family back home, our discussions were centered on how and when we were getting the hell out of there. We would strategize and share any information we were able to gather. He used to quote the lyrics of an old Dylan song that went something like this: "We're always searching for clues where crime don't have no face; love ain't got no business in this kind of place." That pretty much summed it up for Jamie and me.

The DOC offered a program called Intensive Supervision Parole (ISP). It was like being released on parole but, as the title implies, extremely restrictive and "intense." In general it sucked, but other than escape, it was the quickest way to get you the hell out of prison and back home—quicker than any other option. Yes, there were options such as halfway houses and waiting for regular parole eligibility to kick in, but to Jamie and me, it was all about the path of least resistance and finding the quickest fucking way out of Dodge.

Jamie and I had both applied for the ISP program. I don't really know why, but his ISP hearing date came a while before mine. I remember he and I counting down the days toward his hearing and the excitement and hope building up as the big day finally came when Jamie was saying his good-byes to me and the guys in our tier.

As is the norm when leaving prison, he handed out all of his personal belongings to everyone, like commissary, books, toiletries, and his handheld prison-issued radio, and off he went. It was about 5:30 a.m. as I watched the DOC van pull away and Jamie waving back with a big grin on his face. Deep inside, I was glad for him, but I was also overwhelmed with anxiety and even a little jealous. So much so that I was sick to my stomach, and I ended up throwing up after breakfast that day. God, how I had wished it were me going home.

As usual, at about 6:00 p.m., we were all out in the yard after dinner when the DOC van returned for the day and was pulling back into the front lot of the facility. I couldn't freaking believe my eyes as the van parked, the CO opened the van door, and out stepped Jamie. A bunch of us guys stood there completely shocked as we watched him, head down, and having to be almost dragged through the depressing double doors of the facility's entrance.

Jamie wouldn't leave his quarters for days but was finally forced to by the staff. It was a week or so later when I finally got to see him, speak with him, and ask what happened. It was really pretty simple. Jamie lifted his head just long enough to look up at me and say, "At the hearing, the court decided that I hadn't spent enough time in prison and decided it was too early for me to be released." Then the worst thing in the world happened. Jamie stood up, looked me right in the eyes, and blurted out, "And it's your fucking fault. I should have never listened to you about all this ISP shit. Fuck you and your big ideas," and he walked away. Wow, my fault?

Apparently, his wife and two kids were at his hearing, standing in the courtroom holding "Welcome home, Daddy" signs and flowers. It must have been horrific for him to have to walk out of that courtroom. For obvious reasons, Jamie and I were no longer buddies and didn't speak to each other anymore. In fact, he hardly spoke much to anyone after that day. He would just sit and stare at the picture of his son that he carried around with him everywhere. It was shitty as hell to have to be the "fall guy," but I accepted the notion that he needed someone to blame for what must have been a devastating blow to his emotional and mental well-being. Wow, his kids were there with flowers and signs expecting him to come home! Just the thought of it killed me.

After this whole event, I was beginning to lose hope that I would be released on ISP, and for a time I did nothing but speculate, obsess, and second-guess my whole situation. Yes, for a short while, it took the wind right the fuck out of my sails of hope and aspiration.

A Dude Named Sally

Well, his name was really Salvatore, but everyone called him Sally. You never saw Sally without a book in his hand. He would read in his bunk, while walking in the yard, and at breakfast, lunch, and dinner. I mean everywhere. Being the classic bookworm he was, he had apparently absorbed a wealth of knowledge and had a lot to say about many things.

I liked hanging around with him and listening to him bloviate about everything from soup to nuts. Hey, he is the one I learned the definition of the word "bloviate" from. He had some great philosophies about life and living. Things like, "The only difference between the saint and the sinner is that every saint has a past and every sinner has a future." He told me who wrote it, but I don't remember. I always loved that line. Another one I've modified a bit is a question-and-answer thing: "What do felony convictions and tombstones have in common? Once they're set in place, they're never removed." So true.

There are stigmas associated with many things, but in our society, not many acts carry the stigmatic disgrace and humiliation of being a convicted felon. That's mainly because there's just no limit to the implications. Although they vary from state to state, the spectrum of crimes that are classified as felonies is extensive. While I was in prison, I began to realize that I would be carrying that oppressive "tombstone" around with me for, well, ever. While I was living my daily life behind bars, it wasn't on the top of my list of things to stress over, but it was a concern. Not only for me, but for many of the guys at the facility who were professionals on the outside, this meant they would be forever tainted by the lovely new title of convicted felon—not doctor or lawyer or professor, but felon.

This is where I want to reiterate something I mentioned earlier regarding the length of your prison sentence. Your sentence may be five years, but you are really sentenced to more than that. In terms of the restrictions and limitations that come with your new title, you're really sentenced to "life." For all of the "give 'em ten years" idiots out there, I say "give 'em consideration" for the diminished existence and uphill battle they will fight for the entire rest of their lives.

Granted, you earned the title for yourself, as no one made you commit the crime; however, I am simply pointing out that when doling out sentences for crimes, especially white-collar and other nonviolent ones, we should be looking at the whole picture. Sentencing shouldn't be only about numbers—five years, ten years, or twenty. When doling out a prison sentence, the entire "stigma" attached to the mere mention of the words "convicted felon" must be considered—at least to some reasonable extent.

Shock and Awe

It was a quiet, sunny afternoon. There we were in the middle of the workday just doing our jobs and minding our business when they showed up. Big black-and-white K9 vans descended upon us with the undeniable intention of delivering a huge wave of shock and awe. They succeeded. There must have been about twenty vans.

These dogs were barking and yelping their little black Doberman asses off. It sounded like the gates of hell had been opened. It seemed as if these dogs were trained to be as intimidating as possible and somehow knew we were the bad guys. The minute these little beasts were let out of the vans, they were stretching the limits of their leashes as they lunged toward every inmate they laid eyes on. Over the loudspeakers, we were all ordered to vacate our quarters and proceed to the yard until further notice. As we stood around waiting to see what would happen next, the dogs were let inside the facility to do their thing. And then it was over almost as quickly as it began.

Within minutes, four guys were plucked from the crowd of us standing in the yard, loaded into vans, and hauled away. It was obvious that the K9 squadron of doom had found what they were looking for, and it was somehow associated with these four guys.

When we were allowed to return to our quarters, I went to my bunk and instinctively looked to see if things were in order. To my absolute shock, nothing was left in my locker. Everything was gone. No clothes, no commissary, no toiletries. Nothing. My heart started to pound as I tried to figure out what to do. Why was my stuff removed and no one else's? If there was a problem with something in my locker, why weren't the COs saying anything about it to me? What the fuck was I supposed to do?

After about an hour of stressing and waiting to see if anything was going to happen, I walked up to the CO station and told him that all of my stuff was gone. The CO immediately turned around and shouted to the two COs behind him, "We got another one. He says all his shit is gone, too." Damn, what the hell was this all about? They seemed almost as surprised as I was about this. Well, the good news was that I wasn't in trouble for anything. The bad news was that all my shit was gone. Granted, in prison, you ain't got much, but "whatcha do got is all you have."

As it turned out, two other guys and I got hustled. As soon as the K9 invasion ended, some assholes ran inside before everyone else to grab what they could out of our lockers while they were still sitting there wide open. Apparently, this was fairly common after major inspections like the K9 invasion. What fucking idiots. Of course I didn't care about the prison-issued clothing, but the commissary items and other meager items you work hard to acquire mean a lot to an inmate. Damn, was I pissed! Live and fucking learn.

Three days later, I was picking up my laundry, which came back to us in big, white fishnet cloth bags. We had to use a permanent marker to write our names on all clothing items assigned to us. Guess what I saw in someone else's laundry bag? That's right, a pair of underwear with my name staring right back at me. I still couldn't believe that some asshole would actually steal clothes and underwear that they give to you. What kind of low-life prick would do that? I was determined to find out.

I hung around the laundry area as long as I could, trying to look inconspicuous and watching to see who picked up the bag with my underwear in it. Bingo! There he was. It was some black kid I didn't know. He was about twenty-five years old and had a reputation of being some kind of badass. He grabbed his bag and sauntered his way out. I followed about thirty feet behind him to see where his bunk and locker were and then turned around and moved on.

After dinner that night, I got together with some buddies out in the yard, and we devised a plan for a little payback. It was simple. One of my friends worked in laundry and another in the kitchen. My laundry buddy waited for this punk to hand in his laundry for the week and then set it aside. My kitchen buddy then grabbed a gallon container of grape Kool-Aid and gave it to him. You guessed it. He threw the entire container of Kool-Aid in a washing machine with this punk's clothes, or my clothes depending on how you look at it, and when they came out, they were a real pretty shade of purplish pink. Excellent!

The next morning, we all waited to watch this kid pick up his clothes. His was the only bag in the bunch with a purplish glow emanating from it. The expression on his face was priceless. He stood there staring for a minute like a deer in headlights. Now, that's what I call "shock and awe."

My POV

The prison experience is both indiscriminate and unpredictable. This is something that cannot be overstated. What I write about in this book is mine. It is my point of view, my firsthand experience, and my perception. My journey is unique to me, just as the experiences of others are unique to them. This is because of many factors, so many that it would be impossible to list them all, but here a few basic ones: The type and degree of the crime committed, the state you live in and its particular rules, the outcome of court decisions, your behavior during periods of incarceration, and the level of desire by the authorities to pursue, aggravate, or even politicize your case will all converge to form your particular journey through the system. The bottom line is that everyone's ride is different.

Some ex-inmates or detainees might read my words and say that it isn't like this or it wasn't like that, or they might say that my depictions are skewed or biased. Fine, they obviously experienced something different than I did. There are others who might not like my attitude or my philosophies about our penal system and the officials who run it. Fine. Surely you've heard the saying that "opinions are like assholes—everyone has one... "

To one and all, I have one simple answer to the opinion game. You can question, complain, and criticize all that you want to, but this is my narrative, not yours. If you see it differently, or your experiences were different, or you are one of those who thinks prisoners deserve to be harassed and oppressed every step of the process, then my perspective will probably just irritate you, and my opinions and words will fall on deaf ears. If that is the case, feel free to write your own damned book.

And as long as we're talking about opinions and perspectives, here's another one I'm going to reiterate: introspection is a beautiful thing. It's like a self-cleaning oven. You can rid yourself of all the muck and grime that has built up over the years and end up shiny and new, sober and clearheaded, focused and confident. While I was behind bars, the solitude and isolation from the outside world caused me to think about my life in a way that I had never done before. When you are caught up in the rat race of life, you are not readily afforded the unique opportunity to sit back and think about who you really are and what you really want for yourself in life. You're too busy just trying to live it.

For many of us, it takes a swift kick in the ass or total isolation to get there, whether it's lying in a hospital bed and staring at the ceiling day after day, wasting away in prison, or stranded on a freaking desert island, for that matter. But being able to candidly examine and analyze your life is priceless. Like meditation. I've never done it, but here's the nexus. During meditation, you're supposed to focus your attention and eliminate the stream of tangled thoughts that may be clogging your mind and causing you anxiety and stress. They say this process can result in enhanced physical and emotional well-being. They say it can give you a sense of calm, peace, and balance that benefits your overall health. Whether you call it meditation or an introspective thought process, the result can be the same. Oh, by the way, that's another one of my opinions.

Yes, it took prison and a heavy dose of introspective thinking to get me to realize many things about myself. I began to feel as if I had a new lease on life, a chance to start over and put my life back on the right track. I began to realize that the choice was mine. I also began to think about how life can lose its luster and its brightness and fade to gray if you let it. I wrote these lyrics a few weeks before I left the state prison and was placed into Intensive Supervision Parole for a year and nine months.

Color

*Shades of gray and tarnished steel, heartless as a grinding wheel,
I want to change the color of my life,
Shades of blue, I'm dreaming of, a distant taste of faded love,
I want to change the color of my life,*

*Shades of black and shades of white, I heard an angel's voice last night,
I want to change the color of my life,
Shades of red like roses bloom, a crimson veil upon my room,
I want to change the color of my life,*

*Fading to gray, as the years pass away, they say everything old becomes new,
Hold out your hand, draw a line in the sand, you know everyone's waiting on you,
Picture yourself, on the shore of a river, that's shimmering yellow and blue,
Searching for miracles, just like a child, I believe it's true,*

*Shades of summer days in June, rocking on a silver spoon,
I want to change the color of my life,
Shades of passage through the years, casting shadows, waking tears,
I want to change the color of my life.*

*We blew away the clouds and stood there staring at the sun,
never really knowing what we would become,
We saw the morning shining through the grass all covered with rain,
and watched the colors dance across your window pane.*

"Nunya"

Everyone called this guy Cody. He was there on drug possession charges. He was one of the craziest characters I had met along the way. He was a black dude about thirty-five years old who had the best sense of humor in the world. If he ever did get the hell out of there, I'll bet he's a professional comedian by now. I never knew anyone quite like him. He would do these one-man question-and-answer routines. They were very, let's say, ethnic kinds of skits, like the one that involved a black cop, a Latino drug dealer, and a gay white bartender. I'm not going to get into the whole thing, but the drug dealer needed to hide some drugs from the cop, and the gay bartender had an idea. That kind of crazy shit. Cody was a real pro at impressions and characterizations.

Cody introduced me to a few slang words I'd never heard before. To this day, I can still hear him bopping around doing the voice of the drug dealer and responding to anyone who said a word to him with "Nunya!" or "Nunya bidnits!" He would have the whole yard cracking up as he strolled around doing his wacky comedy thing. As you might imagine, hearing this type of carefree, comical laughter wasn't very prevalent in prison, which made the experience all the more enjoyable to everyone. Well, almost everyone.

One guy hated Cody. He was another black dude everyone called Tuck, also somewhere in his thirties. He couldn't stand to listen to Cody's routine and would always just sit there with a death stare while Cody was doing his thing. While everyone else was having a great time, Tuck would get angrier and angrier until he would finally explode and storm away.

One day, he just cracked. It was a typical day out on the yard after dinner. Cody was being his usual self and trying out his new routine on a large group of us. Out of nowhere, Tuck jumped up, tackled Cody to the ground, and started beating the shit out of him. About five guys were trying to pull Tuck off while he continued to pound on Cody. Finally it ended. Cody's face was a bloody mess, and he even spit out a tooth. The COs finally showed up and hauled them away—Cody to some version of a hospital and, I assume, Tuck to Administrative Segregation, otherwise known as "Ad Seg."

After witnessing this insane assault on Cody, I was shocked, stressed, and outraged all at the same time. I kept wondering what the fuck this was about. I concluded that it was one of two things. Either Tuck was just completely insane, or there was more to the Tuck and Cody story than we knew. Well, it turned out there was.

A few days later, we heard some news through the prison grapevine. It turns out that Cody was Tuck's stepbrother! For their entire lives, Tuck was insanely jealous of Cody and hated him for being the one who always got all the attention. Oh, and for one more little thing—running off with his wife! Wow, the stuff you don't know, the stuff they don't tell you, and the stuff that's just "nunya."

Home on a Leash

I was released from prison and placed into that special parole program called ISP. What is ISP? Intensive supervision probation is for nonviolent offenders. After a series of assessments and evaluation by a special panel of law officials, a determination is made as to whether you are fit for release. Then, a hearing will be scheduled for you where another special panel of three judges will decide whether to release you or not. Intensive supervision programs emphasize control of the offender in the community at least as much as they do in incarceration. What does this actually mean? It means that ISP is nothing like regular parole, where you show up or call in once a month and maybe get drug-tested once in a while. If you are lucky (and I use that term loosely) enough to be released on ISP, you are subject to victim restitution, community service, maintaining full-time employment, random urine testing, electronic monitoring, and payment of a probation supervision fee.

For me, this all meant a 7:00 p.m. curfew, mandatory employment, paying half of my income to ISP, weekly community-service duty, attendance in weekly AA and ISP meetings, the inability to travel out of state, random drug and alcohol testing, and being required to keep a ledger of all of my daily activities. In addition, I was also required to pay restitution, which was all the money I received in the commission of my crime plus about $10,000 to ISP as a penalty. These were essentially the *conditions* of my release into the program. I also had to have personal references to vouch for me and a so-called mentor to take responsibility for my adherence to the ISP program requirements.

I remained on this program for twenty-one penalizing months before I was finally released from the clutches of the Department of Corrections.

As relentless as all of these requirements might sound, I was willing to do just about anything to be able to be home and have the chance to put my life back together again. It wasn't easy, and it was a mixed blessing. It took time for me to feel comfortable again in public places. Shaking that "watch your back" defense mode that incarceration had instilled in me was a challenge, and I had to psyche myself up to stay calm whenever I was in a large group of people.

On a broader scale, it took some time to come to grips with my new identity. I was no longer "Joe Blow," the guy next door. I was now facing life as Joe Blow, the criminal, the felon, the ex-con. In the modern world of the Internet, this stigma is more deeply rooted and difficult than ever before. We live in an age of instant background checks that have become the baseline for employment, acquiring a place to live, and other ordinary things we all need to survive in this world.

I learned quickly that finding employment was not only going to be difficult; it was going to be nearly impossible to acquire a job that would come even remotely close to my experience and education. After struggling with this, I began to recognize that there was only one way for me to achieve any real success in terms of income and survival. If the stigma of being a felon was going to keep me from obtaining employment that matched my abilities and attributes, I would create my own employment. In other words, I developed plans to create my own business. This would not be easy, but it was the only way to reverse the cycle of useless applications, interviews, and background checks. Of course, it took some time and effort, but now I was doing the hiring and firing. And guess what? I've always been the kind of guy to root for the underdog, but prison impressed on me the importance of forgiveness and an even stronger desire to give people a second chance in life. Without hesitation, I can say "No, having a criminal background does not automatically disqualify you from working for me."

It took a few years to get past the trauma that I did experience, and posttraumatic stress is a tough battle to fight and win, but I did. Yes, eventually I began to take some comfort in the realization that life is a series of highs and lows, and the more diverse your life experience, the more gifted and proficient you become. Only an addict can truly understand an addict; only those who have experienced the loss of a loved one truly know such anguish and heartache; and only those who have experienced living behind bars are able to know the veritable depth of their fellow man and grasp the life-altering effect of being a prisoner. If I had to use one word to describe my prison experience, it would be "enlightening." Even after fifty years on this earth and a lot of hard times and grief under my belt, nothing did more to make me a stronger human being than prison. Hey, I'm sure it's not what the authorities intended when they slapped me with a punitive five-year prison sentence, but it's what they got. That's right. I feel like a brand-new edition, baby, hot off the shelf. To the DOC and the powers that be, I thank you for your antagonistic yet enlightening contribution to my life. Cheers!

About the Author

Donato Alfredano is a professional with a diverse background including music, education, government, and writing the nonfiction book *Be Strong, Be Tough, Be Smart* about his experience raising a child with autism.

Life is full of diversions and surprises, which, in Alfredano's case, came in the form of a five-year prison sentence that altered his views on life and helped him to become a more compassionate person.

By sharing his jailhouse journey, he shatters common misperceptions about prison and the criminal justice system, offering new perspectives on what it means to become caught up in the system and having to endure the worst that society has to offer.

Made in the USA
Middletown, DE
22 December 2015